The Paraeducator's Guide to Dyspraxia:

Clumsy child syndrome or

Developmental Coordination Disorder

Jill Morgan

Geoff Brookes

Betty Ashbaker

Dedicated to all Paraprofessionals

who work tirelessly to support students' learning.

Check out the other books in this series, as well as other print

books by these authors – details at the end of the book

The Pro-Active Paraeducator: More than 250 Smart Ideas for
Paraprofessionals who Support Teachers

101 Ideas for Supervising Your Paraprofessional

The Successful Paraprofessional:
Preventing Stress

The Paraprofessional's Guide to Disabilities and Special Needs
(coming soon)

The Paraprofessional's Guide to Supporting Literacy
(coming soon)

Table of Contents

Foreword

Let's start at the end. It may seem perverse but there's a reason. Let's look at what can happen when the time at school is over.

My son David has dyspraxia which is also called **Developmental Coordination Difficulty** or **DCD**. It has been his burden and many people have helped him to carry it. I couldn't make it go away. No one could. So we all had to learn to deal with it.

While he was at school, the staff there did a lot to help him. They learned a lot about dyspraxia too. An important part of what they did was to apply for and administer extra time for David during formal examinations. It all went very well. It took a great deal of pressure off him and he was able to get the (high) grades he needed to study Law at University. Everyone was delighted. Triumph over adversity.

So he went along during student orientation week to register for the same kind of support he'd had in school. When he arrived, there were so many seeking support for their dyspraxia that they had to organize three separate meetings! There is a lot that we can learn from this little tale.

First of all, it is clear that people now are much more confident about identifying, and admitting to having dyspraxia. It isn't always hidden away any more. Dyspraxia has always been there, of course, but it has often been marginalized, where it hasn't been denied altogether.

But it isn't regarded as a made-up condition any more. It has its own websites and organizations and crusaders. And there are things we can do about it, things that make a difference. The other thing this story shows is that people with dyspraxia can, and should, achieve if they receive appropriate help. The evidence is here. Universities are full of them.

In my experience these are very intelligent people who have an irritating barrier to overcome. You will be able to help them through it or around it. With the support and space that you will be in a position to provide, children with dyspraxia will achieve. You will be able to take enormous pleasure in their achievements because of the contribution you will have made. So when you find yourself dealing with dyspraxia, don't ever think that it doesn't matter. You really can make a huge difference.

Geoff Brookes

Structure of the Book

As you read this book you'll find a variety of development activities along the way. These give you an opportunity to develop your own knowledge, based upon your own experiences, and encourage you to think about what you're doing, and draw conclusions that will help you. We've also included issues you might like to consider as you read, in the boxes called '*Think for a moment…*'

The intention is that you become an active, not passive, reader through the way in which the material has been structured. We hope you find this helpful.

Development Activities

1. Existing Knowledge
2. Observation
3. Comparisons
4. Vocabulary
5. Review
6. Checking Records
7. Our Obligations
8. Sensitivity
9. Families
10. Referral processes
11. In the classroom
12. Supporting parents
13. Documentation
14. Education Plans

Dyspraxia – the Basics

Before we start to discuss dyspraxia:

Dyspraxia has been called many things in its time – including clumsiness, and clumsy child syndrome. Technically, it should be referred to as **Developmental Coordination Difficulty** or **DCD,** but we'll use the more common term **dyspraxia.**

> *dys* - malfunction
> *praxia* – doing, actions
> *dyspraxia* – malfunction in carrying out actions

This comes from the Greek ***praxis,*** which means *doing, acting, a deed or practice.* Praxis links what goes on in our heads with what we actually do. It enables us to function in our world by linking the brain and behavior.

The brain works in a different and less precise way for some people than for others. No one really knows why this should be, but this is what's happening for a person with **developmental dyspraxia.** It's there for no apparent reason. All you can say is that the organization of the brain is highly inefficient, leading to an inability to plan and sequence thought, and to predict outcomes. More about this later, but basically the pathways that messages take within the brain are disrupted or impaired. It isn't any more complicated than that - though the implications are far-reaching.

It has always been there, but the symptoms and consequences were not properly brought together in one coherent diagnosis. We should be pleased that it has been identified, for the condition is a real one.

Who Gets It?

Estimates suggest this condition affects as many as 1 in every 10 people and may be up to 4% of the population. About 7 in 10 of those are boys and are generally of average or above-average intelligence. The numbers are small but significant. You should assume there is at least one child with the condition in every class, possibly more.

Think for a moment…
If these figures are right, then do you think that the other people where you work are aware of the incidence of dyspraxia? If not, then why do you think this is so?

Development Activity 1:
Existing Knowledge

Try asking some of your colleagues about dyspraxia.

Do they know what it is?

Do they know about is implications?

Do they know who has it?

Do they know what to do about it?

Dyspraxia isn't peculiar to English-speaking brains – it appears in all cultures. It's obvious really. The brain is so complex, and our experiences are all different, it can't be a surprise if our brains are wired up slightly differently.

Why?

There is no known reason why anyone should get dyspraxia. It's not the result of eating too much chocolate during pregnancy. It's not a deformity. It doesn't show up under neurological examination. It's not the consequence of some sort of mistake or mistreatment.

There may be an inherited tendency that predisposes members of a family to this condition. If there's a history of dyspraxia on the mother's side there's a 1 in 3 chance of it being passed on; on the father's side, the likelihood is almost 2 in 3. But not all children with dyspraxia enjoy such family traditions and other factors have been implicated:

- o a momentary problem – perhaps a lack of oxygen - at a crucial stage of fetal development or at birth
- o maternal stress during pregnancy, or
- o simply that particular connections between cells are faulty.

The fact that it can co-exist with other disorders like *Dyslexia* or *Attention Deficit Disorder* means that precise diagnosis can be difficult, since the symptoms intermingle.

But the real answer is that it is nothing much more than a roll of the dice.

Acquired dyspraxia or apraxia occurs after damage to the brain, after a stroke, an accident or a medical disaster. This usually happens to older people and the difference is that they have a memory of praxis that they need to restore. The machine may have crashed but the information is in there somewhere. You can reboot. Children with developmental dyspraxia don't have this lost or damaged memory to recover. For them the brain is literally, immature.

Undiagnosed Dyspraxia. Awareness about dyspraxia is growing all the time. As a paraprofessional you will certainly come into contact with it. Indeed you might be the person who first identifies it. Someone at some point has to join up the dots, and that person might well be you. So when you've done your research into this condition, if you suspect a student may have dyspraxia, then trust your judgments and tell someone, and of course present the evidence you've gathered. This is especially important if you're working with younger learners. There are signs that can be very significant, but the advice here about identification can be appropriate at any stage.

There are those who claim they understand where dyspraxia comes from and, more importantly, they offer cures, but there's little substance for such claims. We cannot re-wire connections. We can only wait for them to grow or wait for the messages to find a different way to their destination.

Those who have dyspraxia must learn to deal with it.

In most cases the condition can be managed, as long as it's approached with *awareness* and *sympathy*. These qualities are vital and remind us what your role as a paraprofessional should be, though that isn't really that much different from the role of any adult in a school.

Awareness and Sympathy

Unfortunately, awareness and sympathy aren't always present in that jungle we call the playground. Children with dyspraxia can be hurt by the unthinking cruelty of their peers, because they will seem odd. But you can provide the support and the listening space they need. Your role, which is highly child-focused, can make you more approachable and non-threatening.

However if you're going to offer help and strategies, you need to know something about the condition. So we hope this book will show you there are many opportunities for positive outcomes. Students with dyspraxia have so much to offer - talents, determination, and a different way of looking at the world. Theirs is a vision we would be wrong to sacrifice. But they need our help if they are to make the kind of contribution they should. The fact that you're prepared to read this book is an indication of your commitment and your desire to make a significant contribution to the place where you work. So we commend you for it.

Dyspraxia – the Details

Developmental dyspraxia is a neurological disorder - it happens inside the brain. The Dyspraxic Foundation of the United Kingdom offers a useful definition:

> *'an impairment or immaturity in the organization of movement which leads to associated problems with language, perception and thought.'*

The Dyspraxia Foundation in the US also offers definitions and supports. See **http://www.dyspraxiausa.org/**.

With dyspraxia it appears that parts of the **motor cortex** in the brain don't develop properly, preventing messages from being transmitted efficiently from the brain to the body. The paths that the messages take are longer and more convoluted that they are in the brains of the rest of us.

So people with dyspraxia:
- take longer to respond to the things around them
- have a poor understanding of the messages their senses convey, and
- experience some difficulty turning those messages into appropriate actions
- find physical activities hard to learn, hard to remember
- have difficulty planning movement to achieve a predetermined idea or purpose

No one else can truly understand what it is like to live with a dyspraxic brain, but it must be like reaching out for something which is always tantalizingly just out of reach or trying to pick up jello while wearing rubber gloves.

Three things happen inside the brain:

1.   *Ideation* - we form the idea of employing a movement we already know in order to achieve a particular purpose.
2.   *Motor Planning* - we plan the action needed to achieve this idea.
3.   *Execution* - we carry out the planned movement.
(You can learn much more detail about how this works within the brain by checking professional journals and books, but we've given you the basics here).

So we can dress, use silverware, write, catch a ball, swim. We have an idea and we can think through a series of actions to make it happen. It might be a familiar idea or a completely new one.

A child with dyspraxia may know what they need to do, but be unable to make the thing happen effectively. They can't make their body do what they want it to do quickly enough. Actions can be carried out but not instinctively and with little conviction. They can't be repeated with any reliability.

We've all seen people who don't seem to be able to arrange their body efficiently to do something like catching a ball. Their hands are still coming together after the ball has hit them in the chest.

They might be unable to produce mouth movements efficiently. They can do it instinctively, but they're not sure how they make it happen. So if you ask them to put their tongue in their cheek, they wouldn't be able to carry out the instruction, even though they would be able to do it unconsciously.

Think for a moment...

Think about the sort of physical activities you find difficult to master.

Which activities, on the other hand, can you manage with greater success?

How important are these activities that make up your physical success and under-achievements?

Are there other areas where reduced efficiency would have greater impact on your life?

But dyspraxia can affect all areas of development – sensory, physical, intellectual, emotional, and social.

Think for a moment…
about the consequences of inefficient message transmission in the emotional aspects of life. We often respond to people instinctively, but not only are a person with dyspraxia responses slightly delayed; the ability to 'read' other people and respond will be seriously impaired.

More about How the Brain Works

Most of us never think about how our brain works, but it helps if we know in general terms how the brain works in 'normal' circumstances so we can see where the problems might arise when things aren't that normal.

You already know that the pre-birth growth of a baby goes through clearly defined developmental stages. From the moment of conception the fertilized egg divides and multiplies. Some cells separate from the rest and multiply at an increased rate to become the nerve cells (**neurons**) of the brain – billions of them.

The neurons are connected by nerve fibers (**axons**) to various parts of the body. So each neuron has connections with many other cells. The infinite number of such combinations is what makes every brain unique. Neurons are connected within your brain that are not connected in the same way in mine. Or Shakespeare's. Or Mozart's. Or Hitler's. This is why there is infinite variety among us all.

Messages and information travel along the axons. A huge volume of information comes into the brain from the senses – touch, taste, sight, smell, hearing, movement, balance, warmth, language, experience, sense of self. This is processed, sorted and stored, so it can be pulled out when required.

Think of the brain as a complicated filing cabinet that requires a highly efficient filing clerk if it is to function successfully. This is an extremely simple picture. The reality is staggeringly more complex but this is probably enough to be going on with.

Developmental Stages

After six months' gestation, the neurons and axons have all been produced and no new neurons are grown. Nor do they regenerate. This is an important point. *A neuron that is damaged or dies, or does not complete its growth, will not be replaced or renewed,* unlike other cells in the body. So, if a neuron or group of neurons fails to complete its growth or fails to make connections to a particular part of the body, future sensory information to and from that area will be impaired. It won't work as it should. This idea of connections not quite reaching the right destination is a crucial point in understanding dyspraxia.

There's a sharp division of labor within the brain - different functions of the body are controlled by different parts of the brain. System failure can happen in any part of the brain, whether that deals with movement, speech, emotion. Hence the wide-ranging nature of dyspraxia. So if you're looking for a simple explanation of the origins of the condition, then here it is: dodgy wiring.

There are two kinds of neurons – those carrying messages to the brain (**sensory**) and those carrying messages from the brain (**motor**). Either type can be disrupted.

The axons. After about six months' gestation, the axons begin to develop an insulating fatty sheath called **myelin.** This allows messages to be carried more efficiently along the axons, rather like the insulation around an electric wire. Without it, the messages or impulses would fly around everywhere. The myelin makes sure the messages are concentrated, controlled and heading for the correct destination. The myelin sheath takes time to develop, and this explains why young babies make random movements, without purposeful intent, why young children tend to be clumsy, and also why some professionals are reluctant to give an early diagnosis of dyspraxia. We all go through a stage when we exhibit some of the symptoms, but it's a stage that most of us leave behind as our brains mature.

Look at a baby. It begins by making largely uncontrolled movements, waving arms and legs around without much apparent purpose. Soon these actions are more controlled, and carried out with premeditated purpose – to touch a rattle, to look at mother.

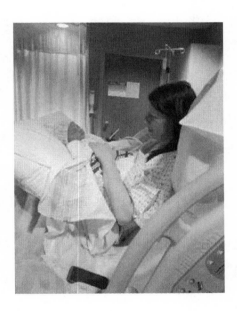

This involves some motor planning, some praxis. The child is subconsciously recalling previous actions and repeating them, modeling what it does now on what it successfully achieved before. Actions soon become more sophisticated as the brain acquires more retrievable memory of movement sequences. It can access these patterns with increasing success and efficiency because it has stored this information and knows how to find it. When it happens properly, the brain's filing clerk can bask in the warm glow of success.

A development that does continue right into old age, is that of the individual cells. They grow **dendrites:** branches that reach out and form connections between the nerve cells of the brain. These do continue to increase throughout a lifetime. Their development is stimulated by the demands of the environment, by relationships, experience, and as learning takes place. The very act of reading this book is causing changes to take place inside parts of your brain.

Unique View of the World

As we've said, every brain is different, with a unique set of connections. These are the things that make all of us so very different and give rise to our personal contribution to the world around us. No one sees the world in exactly the same way. Why is one person good at languages while their sister can barely string two words together? How can twin brothers both become international football players but with different levels of skill? It's because our brains are organs of staggering complexity with an infinite set of possible connections within them. In some people certain connections are securely established. In others they're not.

Disruption

When you consider how complex the brain is, it's no surprise
that a minor disruption can have far-reaching and
unpredictable consequences. A weakness, an unexpected
connection or the absence of a connection between neurons
can occur at any time. If it does happen, then suddenly you're
different.

The more we examine the details of conditions like Dyspraxia,
Dyslexia, Autism, and Asperger Syndrome the more
alarmingly familiar they can seem. We all carry elements of
them within ourselves, to varying degrees - even Tourette's on
a particularly bad Monday. It's all about degree. In most of
us they are small parts of our individuality. They don't take
over. In some, the symptoms are much more prominent and a
diagnosis is made.

Where It All Goes Wrong

Let's go back to the three processes involved in carrying out
an action, because if we look at how an action happens, we
can see where it goes wrong for the child with dyspraxia.

Ideation. If a child comes across some wooden blocks for the
first time, they must gather as much information about them
as possible:

What shape are they?
How do they feel?
How do they behave?
Are they stable or mobile?

If most children are anything to go by, they will also need to find out what they taste like as a matter of some urgency! All that information has to be collected, arranged and stored. There's never a moment's peace for that filing clerk. Then, when required, the information can be retrieved and used to form the idea of building something with the bricks. The child knows they are stable and flat and that they sit together happily. They know they taste of paint. Now, if the child wants to build something with them, he needs a plan of action.

Motor Planning. This happens in the **parietal lobe** of the brain - the planning department that has to plan how to carry out the idea:
Which part of the body should be where?
Which particular muscles should contract or relax?
In what sequence should those muscles contract or relax, and by how much?

It needs to remember the prior experience with these blocks, to refine the instructions it's about to send out, to fit this current situation. Then it's time to send out the messages for action.

Execution. Muscles can only either contract or relax in response to messages received from the brain telling them what to do, for how long and in what order. Messages also travel back from muscle to brain so the action can be monitored and revised. We all do this all the time. And we do it very quickly – and largely without consciously thinking about it.

Development Activity 4:
Vocabulary

Make a list of the technical words you have encountered in this section.

Then add their definitions.

This could prove to be an important reference list for you, not only with reference to dyspraxia but also for other conditions.

The Complexities of Simple Things

When you see the process broken down in this way, it's a wonder anything ever happens at all. It seems so complex. The three stages are interdependent and for the success of any action they rely on the messages traveling on the correct tracks and making the correct connections at the appropriate moment. If anything interrupts the messages or if the brain can't recall this action quickly enough, the process will be disrupted. And that is what dyspraxia does. The delays may be measured in nanoseconds but they are significant because the responses and the function are, as a result, noticeably slower than those of the rest of us.

Think for a moment…

The delays in the brain are not hours or minutes. They are tiny, but significant. What do you think the consequences of such delays might be?

The way we learn things is an ordered process. Certain skills must be mastered first (pre-requisite skills), then other skills are added to them. You first learn to count and only then can you learn how to add and subtract. So any disruption in the learning process for any skill will also affect the subsequent mastering of the later skills that depend upon it.

For students with dyspraxia, it's not that they will *never* be able to learn things. It will take them so much longer, with lots of stops and starts along the way.

Perhaps the information wasn't collected, transmitted or stored properly. Perhaps it was stored in the wrong place. Perhaps it was taken out and put back in the wrong place. Or perhaps the planning department didn't send the messages to the correct destination. Perhaps the right nerve fibers are missing or are incomplete. The messages are not getting through or are not producing the right results. The praxis is failing.

So the child may not pick up the bat quickly enough to hit the ball; they may not be able to work out how to move from chewing to swallowing. And dyspraxia can be such an inconsistent condition. Yesterday the messages were getting through, the information was retrieved and the task completed. They could color in the clown without straying outside the lines. Today the plan has been lost. The filing system broke down. They can't color in the clown. Of course the file may turn up again tomorrow, but we can't be sure. The child may just have to re-learn the skill.

Children with dyspraxia use lots of unnecessary movement. Messages could be sent to all four limbs instead of the one or two necessary to complete an action. Assessments that ask children with dyspraxia to walk on the outside of their feet, for example, show them curl their arms in front of them, as well as curling their feet. There's a fundamental lack of precision, an unnecessary connection that links these two actions within their brains.

There can also be delays in responding to instructions, and poor coordination when different body parts have to be used together or in sequence. Essentially, there's just too much traffic to deal with efficiently, so the required motor responses emerge from this jumble rather too slowly. Information overload, pure and simple, and many of us know how unpleasant that can feel, at times when we're stressed or over-burdened. But remember: a child with dyspraxia might be experiencing those unpleasant and confusing feelings for most of the time.

Think about the different skills and talents displayed by people you know.

Do you think it would be possible for others to acquire these things to the same level simply through observation, or practice?

Signs and Symptoms

One of the problems associated with dyspraxia is that it doesn't have a common set of symptoms. Scarlet fever or mumps are both pretty easy to diagnose, since everyone suffers in largely the same way. With dyspraxia, each person is affected in different ways and to different degrees.

In the box you'll find a list of some of the symptoms of dyspraxia. It's not exhaustive, and having these symptoms doesn't mean you have dyspraxia, but have an accumulation of them and you could well be a contender.

- Irritability and poor sleep patterns
- Poor writing and drawing ability
- Inability to stay still
- Difficulty going up and down hills
- A lack of rhythm
- Short attention span
- Difficulty carrying out instructions
- Frequently falling and bumping into things
- Poor posture and fatigue
- Too trusting, with little sense of danger
- Hypersensitivity
- Socially inept

We may all exhibit the first symptom, and many of us have the second – and the last! But as you read the list, see how they begin to represent a considerable weight for someone to carry. Then give thanks for the fact that you don't have to carry that weight, but realize that for people with dyspraxia, these constitute a veil through which they see the world. Everything for them becomes blurred and muddy.

We started by saying that dyspraxia is about having difficulties with actions, and this is where many of the most noticeable aspects of dyspraxia occur – and the reason why these children were formerly labelled 'clumsy.'

Development Activity 5:
Review

Review what you have read so far.

What do you now know about dyspraxia that you didn't know before?

Make four lists of bullet points that:

    a. outline the causes of dyspraxia;

    b. identify some of the symptoms;

    c. outline the characteristics of the child with dyspraxia;

    d. identify the contribution that a teaching assistant could make.

It won't be a surprise to learn that shoelaces and buttons can be impossible for a child with dyspraxia because of an inability to judge where body parts like fingers are at a particular moment. But many other 'simple' actions are also affected.

Sitting down without looking involves a judgment of where the body is in relation to the chair. As you bend your knees to lower your body and first make contact with the chair, your body gives you feedback – it tells you when to stop bending and lowering. Likewise, a child lifting a cup needs to know where and when to curl their fingers round the handle. He must know how much strength to use so that the liquid doesn't spill – using feedback from the feel of the cup to know whether the grip is firm enough, sensing as the cup starts to lift how heavy it is and how much force will be needed to bring the cup up to the mouth.

If the child wants to climb on a chair, he must check where the supporting foot is in relation to the chair – he won't be able to sense its position. This is because the **proprioceptors,** or nerve endings in the muscles and skin, are not relaying information as they should. Quite simply, children with dyspraxia can't rely on their body. Parts of it so often aren't where they think they should be.

As a result, they find it really difficult to orientate themselves in space with any efficiency. They thump around. They misjudge distances. Their positional sense is flawed. They're untidy in their movements, and ungainly. The child who is always sharpening their pencil because they press too hard could have dyspraxia. The end of the pencil and the paper are never quite where they thought they were.

Those, like yourself, with efficient proprioceptors will manage these things automatically. You don't often spill your coffee or miss the chair seat, and you certainly don't think about it every step of the way. In fact, you pick up the cup and sit down at the same time. What talent! A child with dyspraxia will hold a cup against themselves for extra support and may have to look closely at the process at every stage to make sure that neither the body nor the cup betrays them. And the chair they're aiming to sit on is never where they thought it was.

When I run and kick a ball, or when I'm trying to hang a piece of wallpaper, I don't have to work out every individual movement separately. The action comes as a package and I can concentrate on it without having to worry about the rest of my senses being overwhelmed. I can call upon the collection of remembered actions to perform the task and continue a conversation or listen to the radio at the same time. It happens all the time – writing, washing, chopping carrots.

Things we do every day, that we take for granted, a child with dyspraxia can find tremendously difficult – like stepping on and off an escalator. They can't move fluidly because the messages aren't being sent and efficiently.

Just think of the frustrations of being able to see instantly what you need to do but always having to persuade your muscles to catch up. A top-class football quarter back has instant hand-eye coordination. When you watch them in full flow, their anticipation and reactions appear almost magical. For the learner with dyspraxia learner, it must feel as if the world is whizzing around them while they're moving in slow motion. I suspect that many of us feel like this at times. The learner with dyspraxia feels like this all the time.

> The learner with dyspraxia learner must feel
> as if the world is whizzing around them while
> they're moving in slow motion – all the time!

Think for a moment...

Think about your own schooldays. Can you remember anyone who may, in retrospect, have displayed the symptoms of a dyspraxic learner?

How did you respond to them?

How were they treated?

Do you know what happened to them in later life?

Language

One thing in particular often exposes a learner with dyspraxia: a problem with speech and the processes that underpin it.

Dyspraxia can affect the **production of sounds** because it can affect the muscles that control speech. Then the **organization** of language in the brain may be affected. **Poor sequencing** skills may affect the order of letters in words or the order of words within a sentence. There may be difficulty **identifying the right sounds**. **Imitating sounds**, whistling (blowing balloons!) could all be impossible. It's no surprise that a diagnosis of dyspraxia is often made by speech therapists.

If the learner can't find the right words quickly enough in their heads, their ability to tell a story or recount an event will be confused or lengthy. If they can't organize their thoughts, they'll struggle to establish an order in their words. So there can be lots of repetition, hesitations, and false starts. Naturally enough, if a child can't relate a letter or combination of letters to the sound it produces, they'll struggle to grasp spelling patterns.

Crawling

Just a note here about crawling – which is something that children with dyspraxia typically have difficulties with. There are good reasons why the brain may not allow its host (the child) to crawl, because the required coordination, sequential movement and balance are just too difficult to organize. It involves:

1. balancing in a safe prone position
2. stretching out in different directions (spatial orientation) – while maintaining balance - and
3. coordinating all four limbs (timing) to achieve a forward movement.

It sounds so difficult, it's a wonder so many of us manage it. Never dismiss the importance of crawling. An inability to crawl affects the acquisition of other skills, such as throwing, catching and climbing, and there are those who suggest this early lack of sequencing practice inhibits reading. Many children with **dyspraxia** never learn to crawl.

So, finding out that a child had difficulty crawling could be a highly significant piece of evidence. And naturally, parents are the most reliable source of such information. In the majority of cases, parents or grandparents are the first to notice the signs of dyspraxia, although they won't usually know that's what it is. They may get anxious when developmental stages are not reached when expected:

- The child may be late in learning to sit, stand, or walk
- They may fall over frequently or bump into furniture.
- There may be considerable feeding difficulties if the child can't coordinate swallowing efficiently. Some are just messy eaters who spill things all the time, some are especially inefficient in dressing themselves.
- Shoelaces can be an impenetrable mystery (thank goodness for Velcro!)

Think for a moment...

Think about a simple action you do every day.

Plan out the steps required to achieve the anticipated outcome in precise detail.

See how complex it appears!

Now remove one of the steps from the list – just choose one of those steps at random – and see what that does to the intended action.

Sensitivities

In the sensory area symptoms can reveal themselves at an early stage. The child may have a poor sense of touch – or an overdeveloped one - so certain textures are very difficult to deal with, such as wool, or the labels on clothes. They can react strongly to having their nails cut - some children cry because it hurts so much. Combing hair can be extremely uncomfortable, even painful. Such extreme sensitivity makes the world a harsh and a cruel place, particularly when others can't understand, and may trivialize such difficulties.

Some children with dyspraxia can't bear to be touched at all. Even brushing lightly against them can cause an overreaction. They may lash out – to the surprise of those around them. This unexpected behavior marks them out as unusual and unpredictable.

It might be that they cannot endure holding hands. Taking hands in a circle or with a partner may sound simple – and it's a common enough request in the early years of school - but to a child with dyspraxia, it can be truly miserable and painful. What are they to do: follow the instruction and be in pain, or ignore it and be in trouble? And, of course, other children may feel rejected since they can't understand the reasons for such a refusal and take it personally.

Development Activity 8:
Sensitivity

Assess this section about physical sensitivities.

In which parts of the curriculum and at which times of the day will such difficulties become most acute?

Children with dyspraxia are swamped by a flood of information faster than they can process it. They can't cut out visual and/or auditory 'distractors' from the environment around them. It must be like trying to concentrate on a poetry reading in the middle of a disco. So they may need to stop what they're doing and look elsewhere, to allow them to concentrate on one sound – such as the teacher's voice. Some noise-sensitive children give up the struggle to hear clearly and disappear into their own imaginary world. Where else can they go? The world inside their heads is so much easier. Some learners with dyspraxia have an aversion to bright lights or loud noises. You'll notice this when there are fireworks or at Christmas time.

School can become such a struggle. They're obliged to focus on something that is slipping through their fingers and, at the same time, constantly rebuild a series of individual actions to achieve a particular purpose, working so much harder than the rest of us to do so. It's no wonder they can be exhausted when they come home from school. Everything they do needs a frustrating level of concentration.

What Do You See Around You?

Only those children where the disorder seriously impairs learning or development are ever properly diagnosed. There are many others whose dyspraxia isn't recognized and who are given other labels – like slow or clumsy. Think about difficult children you've met, and you might be able to see some of the symptoms of dyspraxia in their behavior. Children who find it very hard to mix with others around them. Those who have absolutely no coordination at all, who are a complete disaster in PE lessons. Their mild dyspraxia might not be enough to get them diagnosed but it will be enough to make their school life difficult.

Think for a moment...

Think about how clumsiness can influence the ways others think about an individual.

Some now believe that up to 75% of children with **behavioral difficulties** have dyspraxia. Among those in young offenders' institutions the incidence is equally high. Not all young people with dyspraxia become delinquent, but they might indeed become disillusioned with a school system that seems to exclude them, and thus seek other interests.

> # As much
> # as 75%!

Schools need to be aware of dyspraxia and provide learners with the support that will help them build successful lives. In this way, schools shape the future. As a paraprofessional, you share a responsibility for these things. Never forget that you can influence the shape of that future. There's no more important place to work than school – and you have a crucial role within it. So never underestimate the importance of your job or the influence that you have.

Development Activity 6:
Checking Records

Make a list of those children you know who you feel might display some of the features of dyspraxia.

Now check their records to see whether they have been diagnosed.

Ask more experienced colleagues whether they share your suspicions.

Monitor the children's behavior over a period of time to see whether your impressions can be supported.

If appropriate, refer your conclusions with evidence to the designated special educator in your school.

Social Aspects

Dyspraxia is a disability. Even if it's hidden, it's still a real disability. But in a busy school, if the learner is bright and well behaved, their problems can be minimized or even overlooked. For every student identified as dyspraxic there will be others who receive no support because their condition remains unrecognized.

You'll notice that the last item on the list of symptoms earlier in the chapter was *socially inept* but being last on the list doesn't mean it's one of the minor symptoms.

Children with dyspraxia typically:
- o Are less inclined to participate in play, particularly physical games
- o May be less physically active than the others around them
- o Can seem anxious, especially in group situations
- o Avoid physically challenging situations

They may learn to disguise their physical shortcomings by avoiding difficult situations, by being ill during physical education lessons, by developing a deserved reputation for impenetrable handwriting. But the emotional issues will always be lurking in the background, to be eventually exposed by the cruel assaults on their self-esteem that daily life in school can mount.

Early on, the person with dyspraxia reputation will be established as that of an outsider, right out on the fringe of interaction and group activity. They may want to be part of the crowd but don't seem to be fully accepted. The child with dyspraxia learns very quickly that they find some things harder to do than others and even at a young age they won't want to be different from their friends. But they have little choice.

They may find it difficult to build successful relationships within their own peer group, and so avoid group activities, preferring solitary play. They can be perceived as odd because their thought processes are different, making their conversation strained.

> *A person with dyspraxia is often a boy who isn't very good at the things a boy is supposed to be good at. He'll be poor at sport. Even simple things like kicking and throwing can be challenging. Because of these experiences, his self-esteem will be a fragile thing indeed. A cross word or a family argument and he can be in pieces, sobbing. The feeling that he might have disappointed his parents or teachers leads to heart-wrenching and disproportionate despair.*

Being with children with dyspraxia can be hard work. The connections that others see as a conversation develops are not recognized so what they say can seem irrelevant. They can seem out of sync with everyone else, always a couple of paces behind. Their behavior can seem immature.

Frustration and Shame

You can imagine that living with a learner with dyspraxia can be very trying. Their frustrations can take a number of forms. Sometimes they can be physically aggressive, lashing out in frustration at family and friends and showing a complete inability to explain why they have acted as they have. They demand the sort of patience that comes from knowledge and understanding. Sometimes parents haven't got all the information they need. A paraprofessional could be just the person to help them acquire it. But the child with dyspraxia learns to live with shame because of their inability to carry out everyday tasks that the rest of their peers appear to manage instinctively.

Development Activity 7:
Our Obligations

Think about the following questions and write a brief statement for your line manager in which you outline your own point of view.

Do we have a moral obligation to help learners with dyspraxia?

Why should we act to address some of the consequences of dyspraxia?

Wouldn't it be cheaper just to ignore it and thus save money by employing fewer teaching assistants?

If we cannot cure dyspraxia then wouldn't it be better to ignore it and concentrate on other conditions?

Families

Families will need help in dealing with the misunderstandings of the ill-informed who may label their child as lazy or difficult.

- ✓ They'll need reassurance and strategies.
- ✓ They'll need to know someone is interested; that they can put the difficulties they're facing as a family into a context.
- ✓ They'll need to know someone cares and recognizes the positive qualities in their child.
- ✓ In short, they might need an advocate.

Family is generally very important to the child with dyspraxia, as a source of security and happiness, a haven from a complex and confusing world. This isn't always the case, and a child with dyspraxia can certainly create tensions within a family because they're so demanding. They need extra attention and their parents will need to act as intermediaries between them and the outside world in a more sustained way than with their other children. Other family members will need to understand the full implications of the condition, because although it only directly affects one child, the knock-on effects impact on all family members. It's inevitable. But knowledge could defuse jealousy.

You'll find some suggestions in the box for ways in which you can support parents and families.

- Let the parents know that routine and careful planning at home will be very valuable.

- A simple series of graded exercises could be proposed, for example walking between two lines about a foot apart. This will help coordination and could be part of a game for everyone, not just a child with dyspraxic tendencies. Then they could move on to riding a scooter between the lines. This can take on a more imaginative dimension if the path is imagined as the route to a special place or the route to a reward.

- The most important question parents will have is whether their child will ever grow out of their dyspraxia. Your professional responsibility is to be honest. Over time they'll generally learn to adapt their behavior to accommodate the difficulties they have. They'll learn to live with them and manage them, if they get the right help.

- It's pretty clear that as a paraprofessional you're not going to know about some of the symptoms the child has displayed. They'll have happened at times and in places when you weren't around. So if you have a chance, find out more details about the developmental stages the child has gone through. Find out about their past so you know how to help them move on.

- Helping parents find the label for their child's difficulties is often vital. Knowing it has a history and that others have it offers real reassurance. Parents discover their child isn't a freak after all. There are books about it, and once it's been identified, they know which part of the shelves to look at. They can search the internet, talk to others. Never underestimate how reassuring that can be.

A child with dyspraxia might, in fact, be happiest when at home. It's a predictable environment, safe and controlled. This is quite a contrast with the attitude of many other teenagers, who try to distance themselves from their parents. It's something else that marks learners with dyspraxia as different.

The real world can be so frustrating and depressing, the child with dyspraxia may retreat from it and inhabit a fantasy world or a world of endless plans. What will happen in the future? What they will do? What they will become? This focus on the future as a means of escape doesn't mean they're ever likely to achieve these things. It's an imaginary world, peopled by imaginary friends, full of easy successes. There'll be no realistic consideration of the practicalities or strategies to achieve goals and realize plans.

So it's important to encourage them to focus on the present. It's achievement now that could make the future attainable. Plans need to be turned into reality, and the only way that will happen is through organization and planning – and, as we've noted, the child with dyspraxia will need help to do this. Of course, in this they are no different from many of their peers. But with the person who has dyspraxia it co-exists with so many other symptoms and difficulties.

Being Different

A child with dyspraxia is different, and the condition affects every facet of the learner's life. It goes way beyond inabilities with words or pens or physical movement. It might begin with movement but it will impact most profoundly on communication, and social and emotional development. It's in these areas that parents need to confront major problems and fears.

Children with dyspraxia are emotionally fragile and can be easily hurt. A harsh or unkind word expressed in the heat of the moment can have a disproportionate effect.

Think for a moment...

What sort of comments would you find most hurtful?

How would you react to them?

Their interest and knowledge can be unexpected and astonishing. They can become almost obsessive about a topic or issue to the extent that it can dominate their lives. Yet they can't always show enough concentration to achieve in a conventional sense in school.

The emotional immaturity that comes with dyspraxia can extend childhood well into the teenage years. A child with dyspraxia gives you unconditional love and relies entirely on home. This suits some parents, who may not want their child to fly the nest. Others will be forever worried about the sort of future their child will be able to create for themselves.

All this is a genuine frustration for parents, for such developmental problems can seem to be a punishment for having a high IQ. They might have to work extremely hard to convince others that their child has talents and abilities. As an informed adult it can be part of your role to offer reassurance, knowledge, sympathy and solutions.

We didn't know what our son's problem was, but we knew he had one. We became very irritated with those who told us we were just over-anxious parents. We knew nothing about dyspraxia until an old and wise speech therapist diagnosed it within about 30 seconds of meeting our son. Then everything fell into place.

The problem we had was that no one would listen to us when we said something wasn't quite right. And, surely, no one is in a better place to see these things than parents. I know you don't need professional qualifications to become one, but being a parent does give you some insight into your own child. Don't ever ignore what parents say. Don't ever be part of a conspiracy that dismisses a parent's opinions out of hand. Yes, we may appear over-anxious, even fussy but there might be a very good reason for our anxiety, and who are you to dismiss it?

If you think back to your own schooldays, you'll probably remember an odd boy who didn't quite fit in, who was laughed at or picked on. Perhaps you knew someone who took his bag away and hid it. But his bag was not his only burden. He was probably carrying dyspraxia around with him too.

Their intelligence makes them acutely aware of the implications of their condition. They know they can't do things that others can. Their world-view can become dominated by a sense of inadequacy. You need to make sure that they keep on trying.

Being a Paraprofessional

Let's examine the precise implications of your job title, because it's instructive and very revealing: 'paraprofessional.' You're employed to assist with teaching, to ensure that teaching, and therefore learning, takes place in a productive atmosphere.

You're an intermediary. You're the filter, you're a channel through which learning flows. You reshape and reconfigure. You put things into different words. You can reinforce learning at another place and another time. You might thus in some senses become an additional presenter of this material. But there's no way in which you are a teacher. You should have something to offer about how it's presented, but the decisions made by a teacher on the basis of their professional expertise are not yours. Work *with* them.

In case you needed reminding, working with children, in whatever capacity, is more than just a job. Teachers and paraprofessionals have the opportunity, through their understanding and sympathy, to influence lives in radical ways. So look at your title. You're not 'just a para,' employed to clean the white board. You're a para*professional* and your job is to work alongside a professional and contribute to effective teaching and learning. You don't just make coffee; you change lives. This is why you chose the job and this is why you keep on doing it. Never regard yourself as an unimportant cog in the wheel. Learners with dyspraxia and their families need the skills and understanding you can offer.

Development Activity 9:
Families

Consider the comments here about families.

What do you think would be the major difficulties facing a family
with a child with dyspraxia?

Patience and Commitment

First and foremost you will need **patience**. Supporting and
teaching learners with dyspraxia and their sometimes
skeptical teachers isn't easy. There are no overnight
solutions. Small steps, tiny triumphs, but they go together
eventually to make something bigger and ultimately
significant. You need to keep in mind the idea of an
unconventionally wired brain. The information or the
knowledge of how to carry out a specific action is in there
somewhere. It's just been stored in the wrong drawer. And
you'll never find your socks if you put them in your pants
drawer.

Perhaps this silly analogy can point us towards something
sensible. You might be able to stop putting your socks in the
wrong drawer if it's clearly labeled. That is what children
with dyspraxia sometimes need. Basic organization. Simple
solutions. But they need other people to help them find such
solutions. That's what you do.

You'll need to show **commitment** to all the learners assigned to you, even the ones you don't like. It's a professional job and requires a professional attitude. You're in this for the long haul.

You must have **belief**. Believe that you're doing an important job. You may not see instant results but you need to realize in the long term you will have an impact. Always believe that what you are doing truly matters.

You must show **imagination**. Look for interesting new ways to deal with problems. Just because something worked once with one learner that's no guarantee it'll work again. Don't stagnate - keep your brain alive.

A paraprofessional will need to display **courage**. There will be those who say dyspraxia isn't a real condition. You'll need to defend that particular corner and also stand up for the learner with dyspraxia among their peers if necessary.

You must show a willingness to **involve yourself** in all aspects of the person with dyspraxia education, even in those areas where you feel less confident, ICT for example. Involvement will set an excellent example to the learner and perhaps encourage them to get more involved too. You are a full part of the school.

Be **analytical**. Look at what's happening around you in school and assess how this is impacting on these learners. Then think about how you can make things more successful.

Organization at a personal level is important. If you're offering advice to others on the importance of organization, you need to show this quality yourself. So always be punctual; always have a pen; always know what's going on.

Resilience is a key quality. Remain convinced about what you're doing even when the pupil you're investing so much time and energy in is rejecting what you have to offer. There might be reasons for this. So you just have to keep going back for more.

Above all, you'll need to show a desire to **learn**. This is definitely what the best teachers do. Every day they learn something they can apply to their job. You should be no different. Carry on reading this book and think carefully about what you've read. Apply what you've read to real-life learners. Then you'll be doing the job you signed up for.

These are important qualities that help you to be successful in your job and help you become an accepted part of the place where you work.

In some schools paraprofessionals are known as 'aunties.' In one school they're known as 'The Care Bears.' Very nice, but there's more to the job than turning up in history and writing stuff down from the blackboard because Jamie or Jordan can't be bothered. You must always be more than the indulgent older brother or sister – or auntie. Yes, you have to support your identified learners, and that support breeds sympathy and sometimes affection, but it must also go beyond making them feel comfortable. All learners need to be challenged and stretched, and this can be uncomfortable and seem confrontational. It's sometimes called 'tough love'.

Remember, it's one thing for a learner to say they can't do something. It's quite another for them to say they won't do something. You help in one case. You confront in the other.

Working with Teachers

You will have a wider perspective because you will see things from across the school as a whole.

I saw this in art and it worked with Jamie really well. Perhaps it can work here. I'll tell you what, if you let me know what we are doing next lesson then I can put something together.

You're supporting the teacher as well as the student. You're facilitating learning, and are doing your best to ensure success for both sides.
Or how about this?

> *In math Jamie puts a blob of blue tack on the top of his ruler because it gives something to grip. It might help that girl in the corner. Do you mind if we give it a try?*

Once you start to offer practical advice and suggestions in this way, they may quickly be accepted. Teachers are always looking for new ideas and practical solutions; pretty soon you'll be regarded as indispensable. You'll be developing and exploiting an expertise which will quickly make you an integral part of the team.

If there's a problem, ignoring it will not make it go away. The only thing that will resolve the difficulty is confronting it, together with others, in a supportive role. It's through cooperative and supportive arrangements that issues are resolved. They never go away if they're denied or ignored. So if you see something that really is wrong, if there are situations developing that you would not be happy about your own children having to experience, you must do something about it. It might not be your job to deal with it, but it's your job to tell someone who can. You're not a qualified teacher. But you're a qualified adult and it doesn't require much more than common sense to recognize a disaster. Bad situations rarely get better on their own.

Development Activity 10:
Referral Processes

What are the referral processes that exist in the place where you work?

Who should you speak to if you have concerns about:

a. a learner;

b. a teacher or member of staff;

c. a parent or care giver;

d. systems and organization?

Are you clear about child protection issues and what procedures you should follow?

Managing Dyspraxia

Here's some advice for any adult dealing with students with dyspraxia:

- ✓ Maintain eye contact when giving instructions. This will help them to concentrate.
- ✓ Explain things in an uncomplicated way.
- ✓ Keep instructions consistent. Consistency brings a sense of security. It shows the learner they only have to remember one thing.
- ✓ Be prepared to repeat yourself - calmly and frequently.
- ✓ Repeat things gently, leading and prompting the memory until previous learning can be recalled. Just as music can prompt forgotten ideas and experiences in all of us, so the memory can be prompted through a rhythmical, phonological approach to issues such as reading, writing and math. With younger children particularly, sing or chant or clap – but link it to a particular concept.
- ✓ Ask the student to repeat the instructions for a task they've been assigned to complete. Don't encourage them to wait for you to remind them of what to do. They must take initiative and ownership.
- ✓ Establish a predictable routine and firm guidelines. Sudden changes in routine can cause major problems for a child with dyspraxia. Your presence will be the sort of constant that will provide such predictability.
- ✓ Expect the student to need additional time to complete a task. This may mean they do extra work at lunchtime or after school.

✓ Stay alert to the learner's needs. They may find it difficult to wait for the teacher's attention but that shouldn't be an issue, since you're there as an additional adult. Quickly reinforce what the teacher has said. Get the child engaged. Once they've understood and started the task, it will flow more easily.

✓ A child with dyspraxia with low self-esteem may naturally gravitate towards the back of the classroom. But sitting at the front will help concentration by reducing distractions. Be ready to force the issue.

✓ Learners with dyspraxia are emotionally fragile. They may be unable to deal with disapproval or criticism. So a careless or casual word could provoke a disproportionate response. You need to stay calm – and learn to manage your own feelings of guilt when an unguarded word leaves them devastated. You'll inevitably upset your learner with dyspraxia at some point. What you'll need to do is help them develop greater resilience.

✓ A learner may be unable to retain learning consistently and the disruption caused by problems such as handwriting, reading and following instructions may obscure the child's intellectual potential. You'll need to be their advocate, to make sure they're not casually and unhelpfully labelled.

Make sure other paraprofessionals are fully briefed about any particular issues, so they can substitute for you in the classroom, if necessary. Keeping a planner, indicating what you are working on with the learner is very useful.

Fighting for the Cause

As time goes on, you'll be an advocate for those with dyspraxia as you play a major part in releasing their potential. If a child with dyspraxia forgets things, it isn't always their fault. Inability to recall stored information is a difficulty in the storage of information, rather than of memory. It's certainly not a sign of laziness. Remember how those messages, like frustrated businessmen with crucial appointments are being rerouted along twisting railway lines behind a slow engine. The child with dyspraxia probably wants to learn things just as much as the next, but for them learning may take 20 times the normal effort.

This is true whether the child has to learn where the pencils are kept, or where the bathrooms are, or whether they're trying to remember the details of Thomas Hardy's poetry. In fact, any information learned may not be reliably recalled. It could get lost in transit for neurological reasons, as we've seen - an idea shunted into weedy sidings away from the main line, and before you know it, men in dirty overalls turn up and take the wheels off and the idea is never mobile again. But the child shouldn't be blamed for this. Of course it's exasperating, but there's no one who can possibly be blamed for what's happening. And this is why learners with dyspraxia need you, their paraprofessional.

The idea of a railway network is perhaps a good way of presenting dyspraxia and may prove a useful comparison to share with a child with dyspraxia who is anxiously trying to understand what is happening to them.

Messages whizz around the brain on special tracks but sometimes there's something blocking the line. So the message needs to find a different way into the station – it has to go the long way around. So when the dyspraxic brain sends out a message the chances are that it either never arrives or it staggers into the station too late to be useful.

Parents and Action

Occupational therapists, physiotherapists, speech therapists,
teachers, psychologists, school psychologists or pediatricians
can perform tests. But it's the parents of the child who usually
carry out the most effective initial diagnosis. They may not
realize exactly what's wrong, but they may know something
isn't right from very early on in the child's life. They might
not be able to articulate it, but they'll know.

Listen

Parents want the best for their child. Why shouldn't they? So
always ask yourself why parents have concerns. Are they
legitimate? Are they justified? Listen to parents' observations
because they know far more about their own child than
anyone else. It can be a very frustrating time for parents,
trying to convince the school that something is wrong. They

need someone to take their concerns seriously. They might need you to reassure them that their child's problem with the labels on clothes, for example, is neither too alarming nor unique. Parents will want to know the answers to many questions and they'll also want to find out what they can do to make things better for the child they love.

You should be able to offer them some understanding of the condition, perhaps putting it in terms they can understand. They might listen more closely to you - since you're probably not as intimidating as a teacher! – and you need to remain as positive as possible. They don't need gloom and doom; they can provide this for themselves. Tell them they're not alone and there are things they can do. These things won't cure it, but they will help manage the dyspraxia and over time lead to some improvement.

In the box on the next page you'll find some suggestions for what you and your teacher can do to help.

What we are looking at here is a severe difficulty, but it's not one that can't be overcome. How many successful and notable people are there out there who are undiagnosed learners with dyspraxia? (Check this out on the web by typing in *famous people with dyspraxia*. We think you'll be surprised). Look at their handwriting. You decide.
Listen to parents. They might not know very much about the secret workings of the brain, but they know their child. No one knows them better. Someone has to talk to them. Someone has to listen. Often there's no one better placed than you.

- Encourage parents and care givers to use poems, songs or games with actions, such as 'Simon Says....' This helps copying, listening skills and body awareness.

- Songs like 'Heads, shoulders, knees and toes,' are very good for developing finger dexterity and fitting the speed of the actions to the speed of the song, as well as for body awareness.

- 'Pass the Parcel' helps laterality by promoting an awareness of 'passing to the side' and then promotes fine motor skills when the parcel has to be unwrapped, with an added sense of excitement.

- Emphasize fantasy and emotional elements of play. The child will concentrate on the artificial world, rather than the mechanics of performance, so instinct takes over, which will make their actions more efficient. And it will encourage success and confidence.

- Modeling stories and actions with figures or toys also encourages purposeful movements.

- Join in with child-initiated activities. Don't always ask questions or make demands, just follow the instructions they give you. They'll benefit from having to direct your part in the activity through clear instructions. They'll see the consequences of the things they suggest.

- Games which include 'space' or 'direction' words are very valuable. 'Go under your partner's legs' or 'climb through the barrel.' 'Get up on the box then jump down.' You're reinforcing a sense of direction and of order.

- Ask the child to help build an obstacle course. The planning and building will help organizational abilities and promote confidence. It will help them learn to judge distances and examine the consequences of what they do. Then the obstacle course will help develop motor skills. You can give a commentary as they negotiate the circuit. 'You're very good at climbing. Now tell me how you're going to get down.'

Development Activity 12:
Supporting Parents

Think carefully about what you have read in this section.

Imagine a distressed parent of a child with dyspraxia asks you for more information about the condition.

Work with the teacher to plan out carefully what you'll say, that will both explain the nature of the condition and reassure them.

Present your summary to a colleague who has only a limited understanding of the condition.

How did they respond to your explanation?

Do they have any advice to offer you?

What should you now do to improve your presentation, before you try it out for real?

And don't forget that some parents, especially those who don't have very fond memories of school themselves, may feel inhibited or unsettled by teachers. But you're not a teacher, and so they might just tell you more than they'll ever say to a teacher. You can be a pivotal part of the process that identifies the condition and a crucial element in the strategies that are put in place.

So What Happens Next?

When a child is suspected of having dyspraxia, they should at least be assessed by a school psychologist. An **Individualized Education Plan (IEP)** will help everyone, and you can play an important part in this process. It will help teachers to respond to, and plan for, children who are often very talented, but appear not to be.

The IEP

This important document will outline the strategies that teachers should use to help the child. It provides a framework and offers practical advice. You should be acquainted with the contents so that you can support the learner in the best possible way. And you might share some of the contents, because most importantly, the IEP will reassure the child that they're not alone (students should be included in the process of setting IEP targets when they are of an age / ability to do so). Their needs and frustrations have been recognized – but also their strengths. It will also reassure parents that their concerns are being taken seriously.

Development Activity 14:
Education Plans

Identify a learner you have observed in the course of your work.

Do not look at their IEP but ask to see the educational and behavioral goals.

Write an IEP for them, based upon what you have seen.

Now compare what you have written with the official version.

What conclusions do you draw?

Staying Informed

Dyspraxia is not an isolated condition. There are students with this condition in every school, probably in most classes. When you think about the statistics, not only have you already met a child with dyspraxia, but also there's likely to be someone with the condition in your extended family. How would you want them to be treated if they came to the place where you work?

How You Can Make a Difference

There are many ways in which you can make a genuine difference to a learner with dyspraxia. We've already referred to some general principles – the need for sympathy and understanding, the importance of sharing information, and of course the importance of talking to parents. But now it's time now to look at particular parts of the school system to see precisely what sort of support a paraprofessional can offer. This isn't an exhaustive list, but it will point you in the right direction. The ideas you come up with may be far more effective than anything you try to copy from a book. So use these tips, but adapt them to suit the individual students you work with. It's a creative process and hopefully an enjoyable one.

We've divided the remainder of this chapter into age-related sections. However, much of the advice is transferable from one stage of education to another, because the requirements for a child with dyspraxia don't necessarily change when they move between schools and stages. A learner at any age could still have all the problems presented by a pre-school child with little or no improvement. Whatever you do the emphasis must be on providing the strategy that is most appropriate to support learners and their learning at that time.

Pre-School

At this stage parents are most worried about the erratic development of their child. They won't be reaching the same milestones as easily as the other children. Nothing seems right, but little is explained. If you work with children with dyspraxia of this age be aware that the feelings of parents will be at their most raw. They'll certainly want to do something – anything – to re-wire their child. We know this isn't possible, but if and when dyspraxia is diagnosed, you'll be able to offer reassurance.

You should propose activities that provide a bridge between home and school, to show that we're all together and all committed to effecting an improvement. This will have a very positive effect on parents. They won't feel so alone. Find activities the child enjoys, with an emphasis on focused and structured play that will benefit both social and physical development. Physical activities are very important at this stage, to encourage the child's awareness of where body parts are positioned.

Always allow for repetition and practice to firm up the skills they're trying to acquire. All these are inclusive activities. Everyone can take part. Success is not really dependent on impressive physical attributes, and these types of activity help develop the physical skills of any child.

- Teachers and Paraprofessionals can advise parents to label clothes clearly.

- The best type of school bag is one with multiple pockets to separate personal items (such as lunch) and school items (such as a pencil case). It will help packing and finding, if things have their own special place. A bag with a diagonal strap distributes weight more evenly than a strap over one shoulder and helps children who have balancing difficulties.

- Parents can be advised to look for Velcro fastenings on shoes.

- Elasticated waists on pants and shorts can be helpful. Pleated pants make it easier to distinguish the front from the back.

- Eating can be a problem. Silverware may still be difficult to master and a child could become particularly self-conscious. So perhaps sandwiches are a better practical alternative. Aluminum foil is easier to deal with than plastic wrap. Firm sandwich fillings like cheese are easier to handle than sloppy ones.

- Suggest that parents provide drinks that don't need pouring. Boxes of juice with a straw are a simple solution.

Much of what you do for the child at this age will provide a foundation for what happens later. You can begin to improve the quality of movement, and develop greater confidence in spatial awareness. This helps to refine and improve the connections in the brain. The activities chosen must be simple enough to allow the child to succeed but structured enough to bring about both progress and understanding.

Kindergarten and Grade School

Arriving in kindergarten is a significant moment for all children. New people, new structures, new furniture to bump into. It can be very unsettling. But a well-informed paraprofessional will make a big difference.
What does a parent want from grade school? You can offer specific and supportive advice about managing the school experience for their child, and you're well placed to do this because your role allows you to offer individual and specific support. So – with the approval of the teacher, of course - your role initially may be more parent-oriented.

In addition to this advice to parents there are some things you'll need to consider once the child is in your care:

- o The child with dyspraxia may have managed to avoid certain activities in playgroup as a way of hiding their difficulties. They'll already have figured out that some things are rather tricky. However, as the curriculum becomes more structured and formal, they'll have to confront their problems, and deal with large amounts of new information and more specific physical demands. The developmental gaps between children will widen.
- o A grade-school classroom is a busy and noisy place, in the middle of which the child with dyspraxia is supposed to sit still and focus their attention. They may find themselves sitting with their back to the teacher for part of a lesson. They'll have difficulty listening and following instructions, especially if the

teacher moves around into different parts of the room while they are speaking. They'll have to maintain attention while dodging backwards and forwards to follow the teacher.

o One of your tasks will be to ensure that messages are received and understood. You'll need to promote focus and concentration. You'll be a mediator. You'll be setting short-term achievable goals to support learning. You'll find that children with dyspraxia enjoy the individual attention you provide and can thrive in situations where they're not competing with their peers. They crave acceptance and enjoy responsibility. Being with a paraprofessional, they can find both these things.

As the child progresses through school, their ability to deal with different situations will improve – they won't be fixed forever inside an unresponsive body. Their confidence should improve, their concentration and focus will develop. It's just a longer process. You will have contributed to this and you can take a sense of professional pride in the positive changes you've inspired.

Classroom Management

So what are the kinds of things will assist teaching and learning in the classroom?

Homework

A common aspect of a student's growing independence is to be found in the increasing demands of homework. However, homework does give the child with dyspraxia some special difficulties. They have to concentrate and work harder than others during the school day, so they may be very tired when they get home. Then they're expected to do more of what they found difficult in the first place!

It's a challenge – because they don't want to be singled out by not doing the homework. But they could feel totally overwhelmed by it, particularly as they're asked to complete the task without the support of their paraprofessional.

The most important thing you can do is to help them get organized.

- ✓ A homework diary needs to be kept.
- ✓ A prominently displayed planner at home and in the classroom can show regular tasks and deadlines.
- ✓ Kitchen timers and stopwatches can counteract poor time-awareness – at home and school.
- ✓ Tasks can be planned and the amount of time they need can be predicted.
- ✓ Tasks can be simplified and broken down into small achievable stages.

These suggestions all related to helping the child plan ahead, but there are some planning issues for you too.

- ✓ You'll need to know in advance what sort of topics will be presented during lessons and as homework, so you can plan the support the learner needs.
- ✓ You'll need to work together with the teacher to develop strategies to achieve shared goals. You're equal partners in this strategy. Without each other you'd be so much poorer and so much less effective.

Writing

A child with dyspraxia may not have developed an appropriate tripod grip for writing. Their grip might weaken quickly or they may apply too much pressure to maintain control. They may not be able to write on the line or keep words separate. Letter formation might not be consistent. Writing at the top of the page could be better than that at the bottom. So here are some other useful hints.

- ✓ Experiment to find a pen the child finds easy to hold. There are pens with foam grips or textured barrels; or try triangular-shaped pens.
- ✓ If written work is too untidy, then allow the use of a pencil. Mistakes can be erased and the finished product will look more acceptable. But aim for more consistent use of a pen. A pencil can't be a permanent solution.
- ✓ Use an inclined board for reading and writing. It helps ease visual tracking from the black/whiteboard to the page because the eyes don't need to drop so far and are less likely to jump over letters. It also eases pressure on the wrist during writing. You can improvise a board using books, or they can be purchased.

- ✓ Fix paper or books to the board with tape to keep the paper from slipping.
- ✓ Make sure overhead lights don't glare or reflect directly on the child's work as this makes visual difficulties worse.
- ✓ Experiment by playing Mozart as an aid to concentration, as long as you have the agreement of the teacher. It might sound unusual, but they do say it works.
- ✓ Word processing makes work more presentable, and indistinguishable from the work of anyone else. Computer skills are important for the future anyway. You'll certainly have to make sure your own skills are up to the mark!
- ✓ A child does need to acquire some facility in handwriting. Repetitive exercises on letter formation can be used as a means of slowly improving handwriting. But writing out a favorite poem or piece from a story can be more fun and reinforces an emphasis upon learning.
- ✓ Be careful about asking for untidy work to be done again. The child will know that repetition usually means something was wrong. It's better to talk about 'redrafting' and 'final copies.'
- ✓ Oral storytelling or having the child record their stories so they can be written a few sentences at a time can be a useful approach. Voice recorders are now a part of so many communication devices.
- ✓ Don't be afraid to take the child into another environment where they can concentrate without distractions.

Scissors

These can be very hard to use because it involves holding paper in one hand and making the correct open-and-close movements with the other.

- ✓ Spring-assisted scissors can reduce coordination difficulties.
- ✓ Using firmer paper can help.
- ✓ Cutting squares or rectangles from a long strip is a way of developing skills. This is best practiced away from other class members who may already have skills that are more naturally honed.

Other activities that support improvement in hand control:

- ✓ Winding a lace round a bobbin is a real test of fine motor skill, and something you can slip into quiet moments in the classroom – during rainy days or at the end of the day, for example.
- ✓ Threading activities can be beneficial and there are many commercial variants of this activity for use at home.
- ✓ A nail pattern hammered into wood in the form of a spider's web allows children to hold with one hand and wind wool with the other. This helps coordination and shows how actions can have creative and unexpected outcomes.

✓ Legos also help develop fine motor skills. Building with bricks helps planning and sequencing. Of course, the bricks don't change shape either: they're the same shape for everyone and your creation has the same components as anyone else.

✓ Hand exercises or the making of shapes with clay or play dough can warm up the muscles before activities such as writing.

✓ Screwing loose plastic nuts and bolts together helps develop coordination.

Rulers and Other Equipment

Using a ruler can be awkward, as it requires the child to hold with one hand and draw with the other.

✓ A metal 'safety ruler' with a groove, or one with a raised handle or ridge, can help.

✓ Make handles for smaller pieces of mathematical equipment with lumps of blue tack.

✓ A compass is another tool that is difficult to master. A blob of blue tack into which the point can be placed aids stability and accuracy, but it may never be a piece of equipment that a child with dyspraxia will use with much consistency.

Sequencing and Number

When you consider how the brain might be having difficulty remembering certain actions, it will be no surprise to learn that sequencing activities can be a problem.

- ✓ Use picture stories and ask the child to put them in the right order. If you put things in the wrong order, your story doesn't make sense, so it has to be reviewed.
- ✓ Have lots of estimating or prediction challenges to hand – for example, 'How many long steps do you think you'll need to take to place the ball in the box?' 'Which kind of ball will you choose if you're going to bounce a ball over the box?' They can estimate and then try! These are important because they involve making decisions and assessing the consequences of any actions.
- ✓ Another good activity is 'Candy in the jar.' The child must guess the number of pieces of candy in a jar, empty them out, count them, and fill the jar again - all good for practicing coordination. Holding the jar with one hand and unscrewing the lid is difficult for a child with dyspraxia, so at first they will clamp the jar to their body for extra support but with practice they should eventually be able to hold it on the table to unscrew the lid.

Music

Music plays an important part in everyone's education. It stresses a sense of order and sequence.

- ✓ Learning to play a wind instrument or violin can be difficult if you don't have reliable, fine control of the fingers. A triangle or tambourine are alternatives.
- ✓ Repeating patterns and structures in increasingly complex forms can be very beneficial and something you should encourage.

In this way, the child could be included in any ensemble work and be an integral part of it. It will make a huge contribution to the development of self-esteem and be important in encouraging teamwork.

Dance

Dance can have a very important part to play, particularly ensemble work. When children move together and then apart in a planned way, they develop an awareness of someone else's movement and must adjust their timing and use of space to be part of the overall design. Memorizing a short dance and retaining the quality of the chosen movements provides an enjoyable challenge, and helps planning and sequencing. It may sound rather complicated when expressed in this way, but it's essentially all about controlled movement.

Secondary Education

All too soon, you'll be watching the student you have worked with for so long preparing to move on. Having developed a productive relationship with them you'll probably feel apprehensive about how they're going to cope. They'll be exchanging the familiar and the comfortable for uncertainty and anxiety. But you can make sure they're well prepared for this major change. The more preparatory work you do, the more successful the transition will be. A positive agenda needs to be established, so the change is perceived as exciting and manageable.

Development Activity 13:
Documentation

Speak to the Special Education teacher where you work.

Ask for permission to look at the documentation relating to a particular learner.

What conclusions can you draw from the documentation?

Can you think of any practical solutions to any of the issues that are contained?

Sharing Information

The secondary school will have procedures in place to receive information from the primary school. This information must be distributed so that all staff are aware. This is an immediate difference between the two institutions. In primary school, students are taught mostly by one teacher; in secondary school they are taught by many. So there are more staff who need to be made aware of essential information. Unguarded comments resulting from lack of information can be embarrassing and hurtful. In fact, a lack of awareness can make teachers and paraprofessionals look foolish. This is an essential difference in the role of the paraprofessional in the two institutions. You will most likely be working with more teachers.

Proper transition planning provides a bridge between primary and secondary and is designed to ensure there is a continuum linking the two phases. You have a huge part to play in this process. With your administrator's approval, you should at the earliest opportunity find your counterparts in the new school and pass on vital information. It is not only performance details that need to be passed on, but also the additional, personal and quirky information that you have acquired that can make all the difference – their interests, their families, their sensitivities. It should ensure that the earlier good experiences are built upon and the bad ones are not inadvertently repeated.

The student needs to know this has happened. It's reassuring for them that in a way their familiar adults are still watching over them. Students with dyspraxia are no different in this than any other. They all have their stories to tell and the secondary school experience will be a better one if we listen properly across all phases.

What the student with dyspraxia needs is familiarity, a gradual introduction to this new phase in their life. So early visits to the school are crucial, both as part of the class and as an individual. Check that it is acceptable for you to accompany the child on any preliminary tours of the school.

Paraprofessional? Or Tour Guide?

Individual tours can be extremely useful. Students with dyspraxia will need to be prepared for movement around the school and for that bewildering and unexpected sea of faces. Introductions could be made, to teachers and to other important members of the school, particularly the paraprofessionals with whom they might be working. And this is an opportunity to locate the important places – the office, the dining hall, and the bathrooms – without the distractions of others.

A lot depends on the induction program that has been established. It might be that significant staff will have already visited their partner schools. This sort of practice blurs the boundaries between the two phases and makes transition more manageable. Paraprofessionals from both sides need to be involved in this.

Development Activity 11:
In the Classroom

What supporting role should you adopt in the classroom?

Assess where learners with dyspraxia sit in the classes that you attend. Is it the best placement?

Should this be reviewed?

Living in a Different World

Middle/junior high school is a very different world from grade school. Some children thrive straight away. Others take longer to adjust. Children with dyspraxic tendencies can take much longer than most.

For those who crave a simpler life, secondary school appears deliberately confusing. Instead of a small, contained area where everything is at hand, the learning environment can be a sprawling mass: more specialist equipment, spread out everywhere; moving around in what seems to be a random fashion. Confusing is added by the response to a confusing timetable of lessons; a seething mass of older students, all who know where they are going. So unlike the simpler and neater world of elementary school. Personal space will not be constant. There will be more than one table or desk where learning can take place.

We want our schools to be interesting and challenging places. Exciting. Vibrant. Yet that also means more opportunities for confusion for a child with dyspraxia. Nothing seems certain any more. There seems to be less for them to hold on to.

Teachers

And then there are so many teachers. And it would not be unusual if they were meeting male teachers for the first time. Some of these teachers may not have any understanding of, or sympathy for, dyspraxia. They may deal rather harshly with a child they regard as lazy or obstructive. Then there might be a substitute teacher covering for someone familiar. Or a teacher who doesn't teach the class very often – say, once a week. The gap between lessons can make the work too confusing and too forgettable. Different faces, different rooms, different tolerances, different expectations.

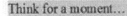

Think for a moment...

Of the teachers who work in your school, who do you think is most sympathetic towards learners with dyspraxia?

Who is the most unsympathetic?

What reasons do you have for these opinions?

Why do you think these teachers behave in this way?

Getting Lost

The child with dyspraxia may feel disoriented and get lost, arriving late to lessons. It will take them much longer to internalize a map and to pattern their movements round the school. Teachers they don't know may yell at them for being in the wrong place when they don't even know where the right place is. School can seem unfriendly and intimidating, a place designed to be deliberately confusing, a noisy shapeless threat, and full of new and unsympathetic demons.

Handwriting

One thing to remember is that time is made available in the primary school for the development of basic skills like handwriting, but that as learners get older there is often no time set aside for these things. The assumption is made that these skills have been acquired already, and if they haven't, then they can't be improved. What the school requires from handwriting is speed and legibility. You can find the time needed to practice handwriting. However much word processors appear to dominate, they have yet to replace handwriting completely.

It doesn't have to be repetitive exercises in letter formation. It could be the copying out of an important piece of text or an interesting news item. Pursue that interest in the wider world and it will reinforce an enthusiasm or interest with your help. It might be flags or coins or cars. Essentially, what you are doing is giving space and time. There is nothing that is more precious and nothing more important.

Subject Areas

Each subject area brings its own expectations and rules – and therefore its own particular difficulties for a learner with dyspraxia. In this section we outline specific ideas you may find useful as you provide support in a secondary school. We can't cover all possibilities, so this is just a flavor. Use your imagination to develop or adapt strategies that will help the particular learner to whom you are assigned.

Science

Here the seating available, particularly in a lab, can make life very difficult for a child with poor balance. They may have to concentrate so much on maintaining their balance on a lab stool, they have no idea what's going on in the lesson.

- ✓ It might be better for them to stand during any experiments.
- ✓ It might be better to let them watch an experiment rather than expose them to danger and ridicule.

Children with dyspraxia need to be part of a team, and the acceptance that this represents. With your help they can find an important role in group activities. They might begin by recording results, but once they're involved their role can develop. They can bring lots of positive elements to group work, because they interpret the world in a different way. It gives them unexpected insights and eventually in this way in which they can establish credibility with other students.

Drama

Drama can help enormously. The bright lights of a stage might be too uncomfortable but the opportunity to work behind the scenes in productions or to be involved in improvisation in lessons will help raise self-esteem. Students with dyspraxia generally want to be involved and like the idea of teamwork. They can be extremely useful production assistants. This can give them pleasure and status. They will learn the importance of schedules and timing and clear preparation and organization. It's something significant and exciting they can be part of.

English

English literature has significant emotional content, and can provide opportunities for expressing personal feelings and empathy with characters and situations. It's important to encourage an examination of the feelings of others in the controlled environment that a book provides. An opportunity to focus on ideas and opinions and contribute on an equal footing in oral exercises is something they'll appreciate. Look for different ways of presenting and recording achievement using technology. The sort of issues that are dealt with in English lessons will provide a paraprofessional with fruitful opportunities for discussion. The opportunity to write about themselves could be very revealing.

Design Technology

The obvious practical emphasis of this subject makes it fraught with difficulty. Inadequate control and manipulation can place us on the cusp of disaster. The prospect of a child with dyspraxia with a sharp knife in one hand and a slippery onion in the other can send shivers running down your spine, as can the image of the workshop technician running for the first aid box while the paraprofessional tries to staunch the flow.

Once again, the opportunity for teamwork could be very important here. The child with dyspraxia may not have the appropriate manual dexterity but there are contributions they can make when they're part of a problem-solving team. They'll have insights and solutions because they are indeed different. Contributing towards the successful achievement of an objective will help to build bridges between themselves and others.

Math

In Math the child with dyspraxia may find it hard to line up columns of figures in order to do calculations.

✓ Make sure they have access to squared paper to stop figures becoming transposed.

✓ Remember that any activity involving scissors could prove exceedingly difficult to perform with any accuracy or precision, as could tracing or mirror work. The difficulties noted in the primary sector don't suddenly go away.

Physical Education

Physical Ed can be a nightmare for the child with dyspraxia, and could be one of the most stressful times of their week. Other children around them will be achievers and may have an instinctive grasp of the skills needed to play games. The child with dyspraxia will stand out: certainly ungainly, possibly inept. Their inability will have inevitable consequences. In team games they'll be the last to be picked. In the changing room they may well be the first to be picked on.

But PE can do a great deal to improve handwriting through the use of directional games, reinforcing the concept of left-to-right movement. It will also help with the concepts of order and direction. So you have a huge job to do here, in tandem with the teacher. The support you offer is vital. The learner you're supporting will need to establish a healthy physical future and if they reject PE completely, they might struggle to do so, with all the problems that this might imply.

The PE lesson can hang over them like a black cloud – a constant and public reminder of their inabilities. They won't be indifferent to PE; they will hate it. They will avoid it at any cost, truanting from school if that is the only way to escape the humiliation.

Locker rooms will require careful supervision to prevent intimidation and humiliation. You may not be allowed in the locker room, but once you've established a trusting relationship, the learner will tell you if there are difficulties. Your job then is to tell someone.

Ball skills may be non-existent: kicking a ball will be very difficult, as will directing it accurately and judging how hard the ball needs to be kicked.

- ✓ Skills can be improved by using a large foam ball to show direction and the amount of force required.
- ✓ Climbing onto benches and apparatus can be daunting.
- ✓ Take them for quiet and private practice away from unsympathetic eyes at alternative times, not just in scheduled lessons.

You may not be trained to undertake specialist activities like swimming, but there are other simpler – and enjoyable – things you can do. Be flexible. Be imaginative. Better doing this than sitting in an unproductive lesson. Take them away and do something better.

- ✓ Music helps by giving a structure to movement and so helps with the rhythm required for efficient handwriting.
- ✓ Bowling can be beneficial. Rolling a ball to knock down pins helps aim and coordination. Alleys can be constructed with benches to contain the ball so poor aim isn't immediately apparent. Pins can be made from plastic bottles half-filled with sand, or water if the game is outside. Younger children can have lighter pins which topple more easily.
- ✓ Basketball can be fun and helpful. Waste paper baskets tied to wall bars are excellent for learning to aim and developing a sense of distance and direction. The distance between the child and the basket can, naturally, be varied and a competitive element can be included.

You'll be able to offer the PE department advice about dyspraxia. These learners must get attention, and should be given significant tasks to perform in lessons. They could become the trusted companion with important responsibilities: the kit-manager, and the scorer to the team. But if they're ignored and marginalized, the institution will be complicit in the resulting bullying.

Tests, Quizzes and Examinations

The nature of examinations doesn't play to the strengths of a
student with dyspraxia – the pressure to work quickly, to plan
and organize, are precisely the things they always need help
with. They may find it hard to recall information in the
correct order. They may struggle to write quickly and legibly.
Unfortunately formal assessment plays a huge part in
education, and the results are extremely influential,
determining jobs, careers, further education. They are the
focal point for most of the teaching that any child receives,
especially in the secondary years. Your job is to help the
learner achieve results that confirm their abilities rather than
reveal their dyspraxia. The student who wants to succeed and
feels positive because of the support they've received in
school will be best placed to achieve in examinations.
The learner with dyspraxia will need help to organize and to
plan. This has to be a central message in everything to do
with dyspraxia. They have difficulty in doing this, so you
need to get involved and help them. After all, the secret to
examination success at any age lies in careful preparations.
 They must learn to take responsibility for themselves, but
they will need your support. Here are some things that you
can do:

- ✓ Help to create a study program/timetable in the run-up
  to the examinations.
- ✓ Include a variety of activities on the timetable. Shorter
  intense periods will be more productive than longer,
  less targeted study sessions for a student who finds it
  difficult to concentrate.

✓ Encourage the use of highlighters to mark notes.
✓ Establish a set of internet resources to add variety and visual interest.

Coursework will always play to the strengths of the dyspraxic student, especially in the age of computers, and this can help compensate for underachievement in timed examinations.

✓ If possible, be involved in field trips. You will be able to support the learner in an unfamiliar environment, and you'll be better informed on the subject matter.
✓ Make use of a variety of study skills methods: relating knowledge to visual clues by designing world maps or spider diagrams; making recordings of study material using the student's own digital device.

For the examination itself:

✓ Propose a plan to negotiate the entire exam. Indicate the order in which questions should be attempted.
✓ Plan how they can use the available time - how long should be spent on particular questions. With the teacher's permission you could write out a time plan and display it at the front of the examination room for everyone's benefit, e.g. '10:10 start question 2. 10:35 start question 3.'
✓ Try to ensure someone is outside the examination room to offer reassurance and calm apprehensive students as they enter the room.
✓ Check that the necessary equipment has been brought.

- ✓ For some students with dyspraxia and dyslexia, the school will need to provide a separate room, so they will not be distracted by others and will be more able to maintain their fragile concentration.
- ✓ It's vital that examination proctors are fully informed about the students with dyspraxia and their entitlement to extra time.

18 and Beyond

Like many young people, the student with dyspraxia might view college or university as a sort of liberation. Finally they can put all their frustrations behind them, forget everything that reminded them of their inadequacies, and concentrate on what they *can* do. They can make their own choices. There's less of a requirement to conform. In high school everyone had to be the same. Now everyone wants to be different.

They need to be encouraged to think carefully about their options. Leaving school is a change that can be managed with help, in the same way that other transitions are managed. The same principles we discussed in relation to transitions between grade school and middle/junior high school apply to the move from school to college. Knowledge and preparation are the keys.

Most institutions of higher education have study advisers to assist students in their learning. Suggest that your student with dyspraxia makes contact with a study adviser soon after their arrival in college/university.

Most colleges offer open days. Encourage your learner to take advantage of these, as they offer excellent opportunities for them to familiarize themselves with the new environment and meet other, equally confused students, who may all be apprehensive about an unfamiliar future.

The ability to cope with others who might be less than sympathetic will always be a major concern. They'll be awash with the same emotions as the rest of us, but less able to deal with them. Individuals with dyspraxia usually react to events, rather than taking initiative, as a consequence of the crucial delays that take place in their thought processes. This means that they'll usually respond, rather than influence or direct, in most aspects of their life.

The student with dyspraxia can seem so vulnerable. Both student and parents will require the support of someone who knows them. It might be the end of your relationship with a student who you have watched change and grow. As a professional you will want this final transition to be comfortable and successful. They should embrace these changes with your genuine approval. It will mean something to them.

Of course it's a big step. But it should be encouraged. None of us should ever accept the possibility of unfulfilled potential without a genuine and sustained struggle. If the student has the ability, extending their studies will be a central part of their development as a person.

Your Job and Working with Teachers

Let's examine the precise implications of your job title, because it's instructive and very revealing: 'paraprofessional.' You're employed to assist with teaching, to ensure that teaching, and therefore learning, takes place in a productive atmosphere.

You're an intermediary. You're the filter, you're a channel through which learning flows. You reshape and reconfigure. You put things into different words. You can reinforce learning at another place and another time. You might thus in some senses become an additional presenter of this material. But there's no way in which you are a teacher. You should have something to offer about how it's presented, but the decisions made by a teacher on the basis of their professional expertise are not yours. Work with them.

You will have a wider perspective because you will see things from across the school as a whole.
I saw this in art and it worked with Jamie really well. Perhaps it can work here. I'll tell you what, if you let me know what we are doing next lesson then I can put something together.
You're supporting the teacher as well as the student. You're facilitating learning, and are doing your best to ensure success for both sides.

Or how about this?

In math Jamie puts a blob of blue tack on the top of his ruler because it gives something to grip. It might help that girl in the corner. Do you mind if we give it a try?

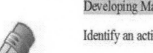

Development Activity 16:
Developing Materials

Identify an activity you enjoyed in a subject that you are interested in.

Get a copy of the teaching materials that are used in the classroom.

Adapt them for use by a learner with symptoms of dyspraxia.

Show your work to the teacher who originally designed the teaching materials for their comments and show it to your line manager.

Once you start to offer practical advice and suggestions in this way, they may quickly be accepted. Teachers are always looking for new ideas and practical solutions; pretty soon you'll be regarded as indispensable. You'll be developing and exploiting an expertise which will quickly make you an integral part of the team.

If there's a problem, ignoring it will not make it go away. The only thing that will resolve the difficulty is confronting it, together with others, in a supportive role. It's through cooperative and supportive arrangements that issues are resolved. They never go away if they're denied or ignored. So if you see something that really is wrong, if there are situations developing that you would not be happy about your own children having to experience, you must do something about it. It might not be your job to deal with it, but it's your job to tell someone who can. You're not a qualified teacher. But you're a qualified adult and it doesn't require much more than common sense to recognize a disaster. Bad situations rarely get better on their own.

Becoming an Expert

Over time you'll be regarded as having particular expertise and this will bring its own status and rewards. You'll be regarded as someone who has a perspective and an awareness, especially if you're dealing with specific learning issues like dyspraxia. From offering advice, you'll soon be the person whose opinion is sought out. That relationship with teachers and your intensive support of individuals will be seen as a means of bridging the gap. It will mean that you can be recognized as a person who is task-focused. Your job is to facilitate learning, to make sure that a learner doesn't struggle so much they become disheartened. Teachers also want the students in their class to succeed. You can help make that happen.

Your role will develop. As a result of your sensitive and thoughtful work in the classroom, you'll be seen as having specific and practical knowledge. It is quite likely that you will know far more about dyspraxia than many of the teaching staff. So you will be an adviser. You'll be able to identify the characteristics of the sort of lesson that will support the learning of learners with dyspraxia wherever they are. Your work will ensure a better experience for dyspraxic learners.

Think for a moment...

Think about how you are going to extend your understanding further.

Is there anyone you should talk to?

Are there any other books you should read?

Have you done an internet search about 'dyspraxia?'

Successful Lessons

So what are the characteristics of a lesson which is successful for learners with dyspraxia? You'll not be surprised to learn they are generally the characteristics of any successful lesson. Almost everything can be broken down into a staged process with a logical sequence. Any process can be displayed as a flow chart – writing an essay, making an electrical circuit, making a cup of tea. This is one of the most important things that a paraprofessional will do when they are working in the classroom. In fact, it is one of the things that you will become good at – and all children in the class con benefit from this approach. Certainly, never be surprised if you find yourself helping others around you in the class.

Expectations can be communicated clearly and concisely. Questions should be asked to ensure everyone knows what to do.

Reading, writing and math need to be integrated carefully into the lesson. The very best teachers make this happen seamlessly. The lesson is entertaining and inspiring but leads to other activities. In the most successful lessons, for examples, writing is integral and planned. Part of your role is to help to make sure that this planning takes place, for those learners who find the very act of organizing themselves very difficult. You'll also need to promote positive attitudes to writing with learners who have dyspraxia.

Keep choices simple. If the teacher gives the rest of the class a choice between six different essay titles, for example, they'll probably direct their students to the ones they feel they can engage with most successfully. You too must consider whether such a wide choice is necessary for a learner with dyspraxia. It might be much more useful to discard four of those alternatives immediately. Tell them they have a choice of two, based upon your knowledge of the learner.

A good teacher ensures that all learners know where they are in the overall shape of the lesson and how much time they have left. They give clear time checks, making sure there's a clock or watch visible: *'There are ten minutes to go, so start bringing this section to a close.'* This is very important technique for the learner to acquire.

The best teachers minimize distractions, and a simplified classroom always helps. They keep screens and boards free of unnecessary information as an aid to concentration. This is something you can implement in the learner's work area. A focused desk leads to a focused mind.

So watch and learn. Paraprofessionals help learners, and watch teachers, which helps you to help learners some more. All you need is a positive and a professional approach to the job.

Relationships

The more you think about it, the more it becomes clear that the whole of the job of a paraprofessional is about establishing effective relationships. You do this in order to oil the wheels of learning. You can eliminate confusion and conflict by being there, by making sure that an appropriate focus is maintained, by helping both learner and teacher.

But obviously the most important relationships of all are the ones you form with the learners you're asked to support. It isn't always easy.

Life Isn't Fair

The learner with dyspraxia might resent your presence as a visible sign of their differences. When you are with them they can't hide anywhere; everyone will know they have a problem. Those around them will know they need to be supported, without ever knowing the reason why. Then the child with dyspraxia can be teased, they can become the subject of unwelcome attention.

Remember, it may not be the system or their condition that will be blamed for this - it may be you. They may resent you, because you have, for all intents and purposes, become their dyspraxia. Stephanie at the other side of the classroom hasn't got dyspraxia and we know this because she hasn't got a little helper following her around. You're a visible reminder that life isn't fair.

Their dyspraxia is like a heavy weight they have to carry with them throughout their life. You can become a symbol of that weight. Like the albatross they yearn to throw overboard.

Building a successful relationship might be a long haul. But you're the adult, so it's up to you to take the initiative. Be ready to be rejected and ignored, criticized, abused, insulted or hurt. But as time goes on, most learners will accept most paraprofessionals. It all hinges upon whether you do a good professional job. Don't allow yourself to be distracted by hostility and awkwardness. You have to be bigger than that. You need to be firm and focused. If you do your job successfully, you will move from being a problem to being a solution.

Remember Who You Are

You're not a teacher and you're not expected to be one, but then neither are you the student's best friend. Don't tolerate poor or rude behavior, because this inhibits teaching and learning. The student with dyspraxia needs to know that their poor attitude reflects on you and you are not prepared to accept such behavior. They are letting you down. If you let them walk over you in an attempt to be friendly, then you will achieve nothing at all. And neither will you achieve anything if you are so fierce that you are scary. There is a delicate line to be walked, but remember what you are doing isn't only for now, it is building for the future and that means that it isn't always easy. It is that old cliché: No pain, no gain.

Development Activity 18:
Behavior

What are the most challenging behaviors you have seen?

How were they managed?

Was this successful?

What did you feel about these incidents?

What else could have been done?

Behavior is important and because you are in the classroom when learning is taking place, then you must do whatever you can to support it. You're an integral part of the classroom and the business of the classroom is your business.

In many ways the learners don't really distinguish you from their teacher. You're an adult and adults in the classroom are, in their experience, teachers. So you need to conform to these expectations. They should call you 'Miss' or 'Mr.' because that's what teachers are called. It might sound odd to begin with, but to the learners around you this is absolutely normal.

Think for a moment...

Think about nicknames. They can be very revealing.

Do the paraprofessionals in your institution have an alternative title? If so, then what is it?

What does this tell you about how they are perceived?

Look at this for a simple but effective idea.

You decide to support a learner with dyspraxia by providing an egg timer. A simple device, but a learner can see exactly how much time they have left. This will help to develop a sense of time values. Suddenly other children in the class might want one too. It seems like a fun idea. Instead of being an object of derision they could become an object of envy. In helping your dyspraxic, you are now helping other children in the classroom as well.

Time for Talking

As you build your relationship with a student, you need to invest nothing more complicated than time. It's the most precious of our resources and you must always try to find some. Discuss school and world events, encourage them to read newspapers and keep themselves informed. This will give a structure for conversation and improve their self-esteem. It will allow them to develop a sense of themselves as an informed person others want to talk to. It's very simple and you are providing them with an opportunity that others around them don't have. Suddenly they're different – but for positive reasons.

Never forget: such a relationship with a sympathetic adult might be an effective substitute for more challenging relationships with their peers.

Talking is key. Through talking we find out about each other, so don't be afraid to offer a little bit of yourself. Not contact details or anything like that, but things that make you a real person. Because you will be a real person who is not a relative or a teacher, who is taking an interest in them and allowing them to share a little bit of your life. It's a privilege and one they will appreciate. They are likely to reciprocate.

You can become an ally and a support in the ever-changing and complicated world of school and encourage them to look beyond it.
So focus on the positive. Always ask questions like, 'What have you learned today?' or 'Tell me one good thing that happened to you yesterday.' The student with dyspraxia may not always want to respond. They may not feel very positive. But keep setting a positive agenda. Shift the focus to good things whenever possible. At all costs, you must help them improve their belief in themselves.

Focus on Learning, Not Comfort

Your job is to facilitate teaching, and by implication learning. It's not that you shouldn't be sympathetic. It's more that you should focus on the real importance of what you do. Sometimes this emphasis will bring a bit of an edge to your job. But you have to be ready for this. If you maintain a focus and refuse to abandon your beliefs, you'll have issues to deal with. But this is a good thing.

Deal with Behavior

If a learner puts their pen down, looks you in the eye and says they won't do it, this is a challenge you must be ready to take up. If you don't, or if you refer it to someone else, your credibility will be shot to pieces. It's you they've taken on and even if they back down when someone else intervenes, it probably won't bother them much because they'll have triumphed over you. It's really no more sophisticated than that. It's primitive; it's about power and influence and control; and it's vital.

The learner has to realize that when they cross a line in the sand, they'd better reassess their position pretty quickly. You have a job to do, and that job is them. It would be nice to think things such as this won't happen. But they will, and you need to be ready for them. A refusal to do something may be born out of frustration or through information overload. You'll have shown already a sympathetic willingness to deal with these difficulties, but you must establish clearly and firmly that giving up is not an option. Learners with dyspraxia are no different from others in this respect. They might be attracted to the easy option, but a central part of your role is to make sure they don't slip into easy indolence. They'll be less inclined to do so if they're aware of their successes. If you've established a warm and supportive relationship, they'll also be inclined to do the things you ask because they'll want to please you.

A Safe Haven

An idea that we think has merit is to provide a base for all students with dyspraxia in the school. It may support children with other difficulties too and will help to address the initial difficulties of transition. It'll be an ideal place for learners and paraprofessionals to meet and build the relationships on which success will depend.

Ideally it should be a permanent base, a haven where they can escape from the chaos. It could be just a place to eat lunch. But they'll always know it's there. A place where they can access help; a place they can go when the going gets tough; a place where they can escape the isolation of the schoolyard. They can take ownership of this base, decorating it and displaying their work.

Development Activity 19:
A Safe Haven

If you had the opportunity to set up a safe haven for learners with dyspraxia, what facilities would it need?

Where would it be sited?

When would it be available?

How would it be staffed?

Write it up as a proposal, if you think it appropriate, and show it to your line manager for comments.

Students of all ages will be able to meet here. Younger students will watch the older ones working and succeeding, helping to dispel any sense that they are isolated freaks. People with dyspraxia are not alone, and you need to develop a sense of community.

This would be very useful at lunchtime, for example, as it's a time when a student with dyspraxia will be trying to avoid typical situations and activities. Give them a time when they can come and a place where they can meet. You'd need to liaise with the special education teacher about setting up such a space, if you haven't got one already. It will become a haven away from the unattractive jungle of aggressive play or games. Why should they forever be condemned to the fringes of the playground?

You may initially get a negative response due to a perceived lack of need for this type of provision. But if you go back to the statistics, in an average high school (the average US high school has just over 700 students), with just one student in each class likely to have dyspraxia (diagnosed or not), that would be a group of about 25 students – big enough to be considered a viable 'club.' And that's a very conservative estimate.

Children with dyspraxia benefit from having some time to process what happened in the morning and get ready for the afternoon. 'Have you got your French homework? What have you got to take to math? Forgotten your ruler? Here's one – but bring it back to me later.' With an older learner say 'Let's look at what is in the newspaper today.'

Other things can come out of such a forum – an understanding of a student's interests and a means of exploiting them, for example. They'll have a secure place where they can feel confident enough to share their problems and fears.

Of course, as they get older, this time can be used very profitably to complete coursework assignments, because they might need a little more time to present things successfully. So access to a computer would be very useful. Other resources like newspapers and magazines could also be useful.

Behavior and Bullying

A great deal of the daily life of school is about persuading others to do things that they would rather not. When you think about it, much of what happens in our schools is, frankly, peculiar. For example, at a time when their hormones are telling boys they should be climbing trees and wrestling with lions, we try and make them sit down and explore the properties of the equilateral triangle: completely unnatural. It can turn parts of the school day into a battle of wills. Is it any wonder that behavior has such a prominent profile? Any adult working in a school will eventually find themselves dealing with awkward and difficult young people. It is the way of the world. You cannot be separated from these things.

Challenging behavior has as many different causes as there are troubled learners. With some there is social or family dysfunction that leads to a rejection of school and its values. In a learner with dyspraxia there is a neurological one.

Identifying Bullying

In the end, what children with dyspraxia are is different. And sometimes the others in the pack will want to drive them out. As a concerned and informed adult, you want to harness their potential and offer fulfillment and purpose that will transcend their difficulties. All some of their peers will want to do is bite them.

You should watch out for the obvious signs that bullying might be happening:

- o the child walking alone in the playground;
- o the child who is isolated on school visits;
- o a shortage of Christmas cards;
- o not being invited to parties;
- o others being reluctant to sit by them;
- o unexplained bruises and scratches;
- o possessions frequently disappearing;
- o a sudden deterioration in the quality of work and in verbal responses.

Dealing with It

The student with dyspraxia might be the cause of the bullying but the solutions and strategies that need to be adopted are no different from those employed in any other circumstances.

Think for a moment...

What sorts of bullying did you see when you were at school?

Are there any differences in what you see today?

Your institution should have established and clear-cut rules about how it should be dealt with. You need to be familiar with the school's bullying policy. A support network needs to be provided and a mentoring scheme established. Remember, a learner with dyspraxia will usually relate well to someone who is older. That someone might be you. Your job is to develop a supportive relationship so that they feel confident enough to talk to you about such issues. But, of course, never take the law into your own hands, as much as you might think it justified.

You must implement the bullying policy of the place where you work. To do otherwise makes you no better than the bully.

There is undoubtedly a touching level of sadness in life with dyspraxia. Whatever they want always seems just outside their grasp. They need to be protected. Theirs is a hard enough road as it is.

Development Activity 20:
Bullying

Obtain and read a copy of the school anti-bullying policy.

What are your responsibilities within this policy?

Does the policy include sections on the different sorts of bullying, including cyber-bullying?

Talk to learners who have dyspraxia about the policy. What do they think?

Victims

There is a reality we must acknowledge and confront.
Children with dyspraxia don't go to school on their own.
They go to school with lots of other children, and they try to
run where the pack runs, usually with limited success.
Unfortunately children with dyspraxia are frequently the
victims of bullying, because often the pack will turn upon
them. What parents soon begin to feel is that the child with
dyspraxia appears to have the word 'Victim' painted on their
forehead.

It is a sorry state of affairs, but no doubt the issue of bullying
will eventually come your way. Your relationship with the
learner might well mean that it is revealed to you before
anyone else. You might see it in the corridors or in the
classroom. The pencil sharpener that your learner was so
pleased to lend as a symbol of friendship comes back broken,
a book is damaged, unkind graffiti appears. Or you might see
it in the tears.

Why should this happen? Why are children with dyspraxia so
frequently the victims of bullying?
The answer lies in the nature of their dyspraxia, its
consequences, and the way that the child with dyspraxia is
perceived.

In particular, dyspraxia excludes boys from such defining
male activities as running, climbing, kicking. They can
become loners and therefore easily picked on. Where will you
find them in the playground? Around the edge. Where are

the pack leaders? In the middle.

Bullying will almost certainly begin in a verbal format as a response to their perceived oddness but it can soon take on physical expression, simply because there is often nothing to stop it from doing so: Hit them. They can't hit you. They can't chase you.

A child with dyspraxia will likely be regarded as peculiar, simply because they don't fit stereotypes. It won't be articulated in this way, but it will appear to their peers that they have not achieved the proper milestones. So their ability to look untidy, their hair, their posture, their walk, can all flash out signals.

What they are just doesn't add up. Their written work can resemble a disaster; their work displayed on the wall, as a gesture towards inclusion, can inspire derision. Yet their general knowledge can be exceptional. So they might be seen as odd, as unexplainable, as freaks. It is seen as best to avoid them because what they have might be catching. The person with dyspraxia's inability to control their emotions may lead to them being labeled as immature. This can be exacerbated by their obvious difficulties in basic areas like getting dressed, tying laces, eating.

It's also possible that they prefer playing with children who are either younger or older than themselves. Their own peers are the ones they avoid because of the challenges they pose – and they are the ones who establish reputations.

Emotional Consequences

Learners with dyspraxia may seem to be living to a different time from the rest of us - always that little bit behind. This is something that comedians have used for years – the character who's out of step, either mentally or physically, with everyone else around them. This comic model is well established. It brings easy laughs. Some students compensate by clowning around implying "I've got dyspraxia. Laugh at me."

The unique combination of connections within our brains are even the basis for humor. A unique and surprising connection is made between thoughts or events. It's something that hasn't occurred to us before. But someone else has seen it. Why didn't we? We didn't see it because our brains were busy seeing other things. They're the comedian; our strengths lie elsewhere.

It can't be a surprise, therefore, if those who fit this stereotype are derided and abused. They can find themselves the butt of everyone's attempts at humor because they always seem to be catching up with a world that's moving faster than they are. They can say the wrong thing, miss the point, and need three attempts to start a sentence. By the time they get around to finishing it, the world has long since moved on.

Yet it's also true to say that children with dyspraxia are special, with a refreshing innocence and an engaging relationship with their work. They must not be sacrificed to the mindless oafs with an old joke to try out. Teachers and paraprofessionals will need to show vigilance if learners with dyspraxia are to be given the space in which to succeed. Not to do so is to leave their potential unfulfilled and the world a much poorer place.

The emotional consequences of dyspraxia do need careful consideration. The world they try to inhabit can be difficult enough. Their days can be stressful. They live with frustration, anxiety and failure. Their self-esteem can be low. They may have behavior problems that these issues provoke. Being dyspraxic is hard work.

The inconsistent development of the brain can affect their emotional development too. The information they get from their experiences and senses may be impaired, so they may not be able to understand their feelings. They may show inappropriate emotions, or too much. So a small set-back can become a disaster. They can be too easily moved to tears. They can focus obsessively upon events like birthdays or holidays, repeating plans and ideas constantly until they appear to be real. They may pursue the repetition of questions and their answers as they try to fix an issue in their minds. This means that ordinary life, as we all come to understand it, can contain additional frustration and disappointment. These frustrations can make them seem immature and certainly emotionally fragile.

Without the consistent ability to read people and situations or to recognize accepted behavior, friendships may be difficult to form. So on the one hand they want to keep up with their peers and to achieve, but their behavior seems odd and off-putting. In these circumstances, it is no surprise that they are frequently the victims of prolonged bullying.

We must not let it happen.

Specific Hints and Tips

As you will be beginning to see, for some learners with dyspraxia school is a daily confrontation with inadequacy. They know they can't cope very well – and they have to face this every day. Not only that, but they are constantly reminded of their shortcomings by other learners and by unsympathetic adults. Most of us, when faced with something so unpleasant, would avoid it if it were possible. This is how some learners with dyspraxia feel about education: not as an opportunity for success but as a reminder of failure.

There is an obvious internal tension within learners with dyspraxia because of the difference between what they want to do and what they can achieve. They can model what they want to do quite successfully within their heads. They can imagine themselves as achievers, but it might be some time before reality catches up with their expectations – and there will be others around them who won't let them forget it.

Dealing with other people is also very frustrating for them, and their condition can lead to real exclusion by their peers and a similar lack of understanding from adults. If, for example, they have a difficulty in following instructions, a request for them to be repeated could mean that they are accused of not listening. They can become frustrated and irritated by such perceived intolerance. If they can't keep up with the conversation around them and are mocked for their clumsy interactions, they can feel humiliated and isolated.

The stress of being at school can lead to poor behavior in response to such an unsympathetic world. Indeed, some children can display temper tantrums because the world seems deliberately to misunderstand their condition. They might also carry with them a sense of guilt, because they feel that they are letting their family down because of the way others see them – as a clumsy incompetent embarrassment. No one else in their family has such a reputation.
As they progress through secondary school many students with dyspraxia will decide to opt out of education at the earliest opportunity. This shouldn't be a surprise. If they feel that their needs are neither recognized nor met, they can feel isolated and forgotten. It is much easier to be a clown or to become a disaffected isolate in order to hide any limitations and thus avoid dealing with failure.

Recognition

We are always ready to recognize the needs of the physically disabled. Ramps and lifts are provided in schools for children in wheelchairs. No one would expect a deaf child to respond instantly to whispered commands. We would make sure that their needs were met and the necessary equipment made available.

Learners with dyspraxia have the same rights. Their condition needs to be recognized and a strategy developed to accommodate it.

A paraprofessional should be an integral part of that strategy. Through the intensive support that you provide, you should attempt to set a positive agenda. This must be the best way of addressing concerns about behavior.

Support the child, modify their behavior and the behavior of others, and so allow them to succeed.

Organizing

The fate of a learner with dyspraxia is to seek desperately for an elusive moment of calm and stillness at the heart of a chaotic world. Everything revolves at high speed. Information bombards them. Demands are piled upon instructions, in a life full of requests and alternatives. They spend their days grasping at things that are no longer there. To be honest, it doesn't appear to be much different for the rest of us. Our own lives appear manic and chaotic at times, but we develop ways of handling this. We have our own ways of getting through the day. Look at how we manage to get out of the house in the morning to go to work. We do it generally because we are organized and because we have a system. Without it, everything will just fall apart. Well, that's what those with dyspraxia need: a bit of organization. It is something that they often cannot provide for themselves. So you can help them to get organized. And while organizing your own life might seem impossible at times, sorting out theirs is not that difficult.

Leading by Example

It's clear that you don't have to take complete control of their life. You are not some sort of secondary brain that takes over when times are hard, via a set of jump leads. You exist to point students in the right direction, through advice and example. You yourself need to be prepared for lessons, fully equipped and on time, with a clear idea of what is happening and with a clear plan for the whole of the day. This is how you can set an example, and it is important. You must accept that you are a role model. Of course the child needs to begin to take some responsibility for the things around them, because this is the way that they will need to approach the rest of their lives. But a little bit of help at an early age can go a long way.

The Importance of Planning and Management

A carefully arranged strategy by which the child with dyspraxia can confront and conquer the school day will help enormously. Someone with your perspective can help to establish a successful and organized routine. Because if learning is to take place, then the challenges presented by the daily business of school need to be resolved. And without a careful and thoughtful approach, the whole day can become a mess.

In fact, it seems to me that effective management of dyspraxia can be achieved in simple things like personal support and organization. Because you can provide the techniques and the structures that they need and, in doing so, you will assist teaching and learning.

Strategies

- ✓ A transparent pencil case provides a quick and easy check that everything is present, without the need for fumbling with uncooperative zippers.
- ✓ Encourage the learner to have a place for everything and to put things back properly so that they can be easily found. I suppose this is a good analogy for the idea of what is happening inside the person with dyspraxia brain. We always need to put things back in the correct place if we want to find them again.

- ✓ Encourage the making of lists of things to do that are then regularly reviewed. This is particularly useful with older learners with dyspraxia, but it is obviously something that can be adapted for younger ones too. Start good habits early.
- ✓ Use a sloping surface for writing to assist clarity and neatness. An older learner can try this out in a graphics office or you can build a temporary support on a desk from books.
- ✓ Post-it notes can provide instant temporary reminders and can be displayed prominently and in a variety of places. They have the additional advantage of being disposable. Tear them up and start again, or discard them, as a visible symbol of how a learner is moving through a task and nearing its completion.
- ✓ Ask dyspraxic learners to repeat instructions - never assume the child has engaged with the task straight away. It helps if the teacher does this as well as the assistant, not least because it is useful support for others in the class.
- ✓ Once you have gotten to know the learner and have won their confidence, encourage them to join appropriate groups and school societies. It might help – or it might not – on the first couple of occasions to go along with them just to give them the comfort of your support, but that should not persist.

- ✓ Use a laptop or tablet where possible, since it aids correction and redrafting and brings the pleasure of seeing something with a clean professional finish that transcends the vagaries of handwriting.
- ✓ A voice recorder can help in remembering important points and instructions –it makes them transportable and they can be recalled accurately away from the lesson and on other occasions. Most modern cell phones have this function. This will also provide a structure for written responses, confirming the shape that is required.
- ✓ Encourage the child to talk themselves through a task so that they can engage with the different stages and processes that make it up. This will also encourage ownership of the task.

This sort of underpinning will allow learners to function both in school and beyond. To see a role model like yourself giving this sort of advice is very influential. I will give weight and credibility to the advice you offer, especially if you are seen as organized and efficient yourself. You will be establishing techniques and processes that should last them a lifetime.

Be Positive

Emphasis needs to be placed on success rather than failure. Remind them constantly of their achievements: be positive. Your objective must be to disperse the low self-esteem that develops among some children with dyspraxia. You can address bullying issues by promoting self-worth.

- ✓ Make them feel good about themselves by helping them to be organized.
- ✓ Be an organized role model yourself.
- ✓ Help them structure their day.
- ✓ Set short-term, achievable goals.
- ✓ Encourage their interests.
- ✓ Provide a haven for them.
- ✓ Introduce them to other learners with whom they can be mutually supportive.
- ✓ Be ready to express your disapproval of their more challenging behaviors.
- ✓ Act as an intermediary between the learner and the teacher if necessary.
- ✓ Promote knowledge about dyspraxia.
- ✓ Become involved in the lessons yourself.
- ✓ Involve people without dyspraxia in your classroom solutions to dispel the sense of isolation.

In Conclusion

At some point, at whatever stage you are working, you'll have to hand your friend with dyspraxia on to someone else. What we want more than anything else is to hand them on ready to embrace new achievements.

We all need to feel that what we do creates an impact, that we make a difference. This is particularly the case with an issue as difficult and frustrating as dyspraxia. There will be so many setbacks, and so many times when progress appears to be minimal or insignificant. A paraprofessional must inevitably sometimes feel that they are irrelevant.

But a good paraprofessional shouldn't feel like that. Because the difference you will make will eventually be a great step made up of a lot of much smaller ones. This is why you need patience and resilience, because there is unlikely to be any great and unexpected transformation. Everything with dyspraxia is gradual, almost imperceptible. So keep on keeping on, and over time you will have made a huge difference.

We might ask the question: *How you know you've been successful*? and we may have the answer. It doesn't lie in data about performance or in externally verified tests. For most of you there is a much simpler measure: Does the student with dyspraxia come back to visit you after they have left high school and moved on? It may sound rather trivial, and it isn't scientific. But if you think about it, a student with dyspraxia who stays in touch shows that:

- ✓ the relationship you established was important to them;

- ✓ they can make decisions and put them into action;

- ✓ they're confident enough to take the initiative for that visit;

- ✓ they might well have had to make, and manage, travel arrangements;

- ✓ they want to share their successes and their news with you;

- ✓ they have an awareness of social obligations, perhaps also a sense of gratitude;

- ✓ it's not only their teachers they remember; it's the assistant who gave them so much;

- ✓ they are not afraid of revisiting their past.

Your student with dyspraxia has grown. And you've done something to change a life. Isn't that something that you can be justifiably proud of?

Think for a moment…

Consider who else might benefit from reading this book.

What are you going to tell them about it?

Which parts of it reflect your own experiences?

Resources

1. Dyspraxic Foundation
http://www.dyspraxiafoundation.org.uk/

UK based charity started by mothers of dyspraxia-diagnosed children. The goals and aims of the foundation are to increase awareness of the disease, offer support to those living with dyspraxia, educate and assist health care officials and educators about the disease, and to provide better treatment for those living with the disease. Mostly centered in the UK.

The objectives of the Foundation are:
- to support individuals and families affected by dyspraxia.
- to promote better diagnostic and treatment facilities for those who have dyspraxia.
- to help professionals in health and education to assist those with Dyspraxia.
- to promote awareness and understanding of dyspraxia.

Each year the Foundation answers approximately 10,000 enquiries and distributes more then 20,000 leaflets about the condition. The Foundation seeks every opportunity to increase understanding of dyspraxia, particularly among professionals in health and education.

The Foundation is run by fewer than six full-time equivalent paid staff and is supported extensively by volunteers. Its work is funded entirely by voluntary donation and membership subscriptions.

What else do they do?

- o Publish leaflets, booklets, books and guides for parents, those who have dyspraxia and professionals.
- o Organize conferences and talks about dyspraxia and related topics for parents, care givers and professionals.
- o Support a network of local groups across the United Kingdom.
- o Support a group for adults who have dyspraxia.

2. Dyspraxia Foundation USA:
http://www.dyspraxiausa.org/
Focuses on educating people about the disease to increase understanding. The big focus is on helping those with dyspraxia find support and acceptance. The foundation has an awareness campaign and also various "success stories" to inspire and motivate families and individuals. The foundation desires increased understanding among educators so they can more effectively assist their students.

3. CanChild- Centre for Childhood Disability Research:
http://www.canchild.ca/en/
CanChild is funded by McMaster University and is a research-based group for disabilities in children. It is run by a group of researchers from various fields to provide information concerning many disabilities including dyspraxia.

4. Understood:
https://www.understood.org/en
https://www.understood.org/en/learning-attention-issues/child-learning-disabilities/dyspraxia
15 non-profit organizations united to assist parents of children who have a learning or attention disorder (including dyspraxia). It focuses on giving parents access to information and opportunities to help their children progress.

5. National Institute of Neurological Disorders and Stroke:
http://www.ninds.nih.gov/disorders/dyspraxia/dyspraxia.ht
m
The NINDS performs research on neurological disorders, fund
and perform training to those whose careers are involved in
these disorders, and educate the general public and policy-
makers about these disorders. Their information concerning
dyspraxia gives a basic understanding of what the disorder is,
it there is a treatment, what the prognosis is, and what types
of research is being done.

6. American Speech-Language hearing Association:
http://www.asha.org/
ASHA is an association for professionals with careers in
audiology, speech-language pathology, and speech, language,
and hearing scientists. Their mission is to provide correct and
up to date information for these professionals to empower
them to provide excellence in their service to clients/students
they serve as well as to advocate for those clients/students as
well. They have numerous studies and information about
dyspraxia.

7. Learning Disabilities Association of America:
http://ldaamerica.org/
LDA is focused on helping people with learning disabilities
become fully acting members in society and to prevent
learning disabilities in the future. LDA works on supporting
parents, increasing awareness, working with legislatures to
better the lives of people with learning disabilities, and
working to develop effective school programs. The
association focuses on a wide range of learning difficulties,
including dyspraxia.

8. Patient
http://www.patient.co.uk/doctor/Dyspraxia-and-Apraxia.htm
Patient is an online company and website run by doctors in
the UK. It is funded by other sources than website users. It is
used by doctors and patients to receive credible health
information.

9. NHS choices
http://www.nhs.uk/conditions/dyspraxia-
(childhood)/Pages/Introduction.aspx
NHS is a form of health care offered to citizens in the UK.
Their website has information about various health issues
while also providing health care service. It's a member of the
Information Standard.

10. MNT
http://www.medicalnewstoday.com/articles/151951.php
Medial News Today is a medical company in the UK who tries
to find the most credible and up to date health information for
the public. It has quite a bit of information on dyspraxia.

11. The National Autistic Society
http://www.autism.org.uk/about-autism/related-
conditions/dyspraxia.aspx
This is a website for the National Autistic Society of the UK.
While the site and society focus on autism, they also are
interested in learning and sharing information of disorders
that are can be related to autism. They have quite a bit of
information on dyspraxia.

12. Dore
http://www.dore.co.uk/learning-difficulties/dyspraxia/

DORE is a UK based company that calls itself a "community interest company." It focuses on learning disabilities in children.

13. LD online
http://www.ldonline.org/article/14616/
LD online is a site meant to help educators help students with ADHD and learning disabilities. It is an educational service of PBS.

Other books in the Kindle *Paraprofessional* series:

The Pro-Active Paraeducator: More than 250 Smart Ideas for Paraprofessionals who Support Teachers

The Paraprofessional's Guide to Disabilities and Special Needs (coming soon)

The Paraprofessional's Guide to Supporting Literacy (coming soon)

101 Ideas for Supervising Your Paraprofessional

The Successful Paraprofessional: Preventing Stress

Other print books by these authors:

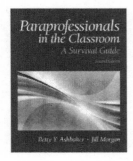

Paraprofessionals in the Classroom: A Survival Guide (2nd Edition)

https://www.amazon.com/Paraprofessionals-Classroom-Survival-Guide-2nd/dp/0132659824?ie=UTF8&qid=1465667106&ref_=la_B0030GCI1K_1_1&s=books&sr=1-1

The Paraprofessional's Guide to Effective Behavioral Intervention

https://www.amazon.com/Paraprofessionals-Guide-Effective-Behavioral-Intervention/dp/0415739195?ie=UTF8&*Version*=1&*entries*=0

We hope you've enjoyed the series of books written specifically for instructional paraprofessionals working with students in the schools.

Other books are available for teachers as supervisors:

A Teacher's Guide to Working with Paraeducators and Other Classroom Aides.

Available through the Association for Supervision and Curriculum Development at:

http://www.ascd.org/Publications/Books/Overview/A-Teachers-Guide-to-Working-with-Paraeducators-and-Other-Classroom-Aides.aspx

Supporting and Supervising your Teaching Assistant [Paraprofessional] by Jill Morgan & Betty Ashbaker.

Available through Amazon at:

https://www.amazon.com/Supporting-Supervising-your-Teaching-Assistant/dp/1847063845/ref=sr_1_31?ie=UTF8&qid=1468503779&sr=8-31&keywords=ashbaker

Achieving Outstanding Classroom Support in your Secondary School.

Available through Routledge at:

https://www.routledge.com/Achieving-Outstanding-Classroom-Support-in-Your-Secondary-School-Tried/Morgan-Jones-Booth-Coates/p/book/9781138833739

Made in the USA
Lexington, KY
27 August 2019